Busty, Slag and Nob End

BUSTY, SLAG AND NOB END

Remarkably rude but real names of
people, places and products from
all over the world

Russell Ash

headline

First published in 2009
by HEADLINE PUBLISHING GROUP

1

Cataloguing in Publication Data is available from the British Library

ISBN 978 0 7553 1870 4

Typeset in Meridien

Designed by Bernard Higton

Printed and bound in Great Britain by
Clays Ltd, St Ives plc

HEADLINE PUBLISHING GROUP
An Hachette UK Company
338 Euston Road
London NW1 3BH

www.headline.co.uk
www.hachette.co.uk

www.bustyslagandnobend.com

Acknowledgments

Under normal circumstances, I would be delighted to thank those who have kindly contributed names to this book. However, I am aware that, given the nature of many of the entries, there may be some sensitive souls, respected archivists and other distinguished individuals who would prefer not to be associated with it.
With their sensibilities in mind, I offer my warmest thanks to everyone who has helped me –
you know who you are.
A special note of thanks to my great-uncle Harry, whose extensive collection of Victorian and Edwardian porn has provided most of the photos in this book.
It is good to know that his many visits to Paris in the inter-war years were not wasted.

CONTENTS

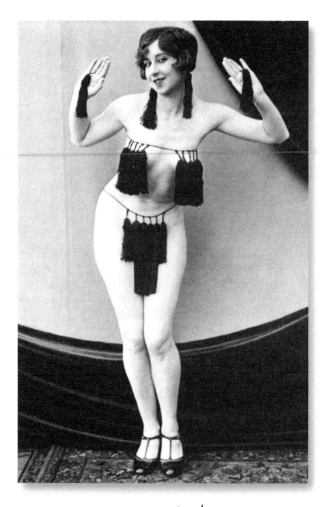

Fanny Flasher

(see page 64)

INTRODUCTION

Naughty names revisited

When I compiled this book's predecessor, *Potty, Fartwell & Knob*, I was astonished – as were its many readers (thanks be to them) – to discover that a lot of people had borne strange names. It was not just the inherent oddity and humour in them, but the awareness that innumerable individuals have had to struggle through their lives pronouncing, explaining or spelling out these names. Nowhere is this truer than with 'rude' names – names that through double, or in many instances single, entendre mean something that a large proportion of the population would consider offensive.

In Britain, such names have long been the subject of some of our most inventive humour, from the fabulous creations of the panellists on the radio show *I'm Sorry I Haven't a Clue* to the sexually provocative Bond girls Pussy Galore, Plenty O'Toole and Xenia Onatopp. Yet no one has brought these evocative names together in book form before. Perhaps those who transcribed the records – and all credit to them – are serious-minded archivists who don't appreciate the richness of some of the material they are handling. I can't help thinking if I were to come across one of these names in some ancient census return, I'd leap in the air and tell all my colleagues.

Turning the research telescope in this direction has been remarkably revealing. The names featured in *Potty, Fartwell & Knob*, where about a quarter fell into this category (some of the best of which are revisited here), turn out to have been only the tip of what I described there as the onomastic (relating to names) iceberg. Extending the parameters beyond these shores has turned the iceberg into a floe of Arctic proportions, introduced new fields worthy of exploration, more opportunities for misunderstanding and yet more astonishment at the sheer variety of names.

Accidental vs deliberate

The many thousands of amusingly rude names posted on websites, frequently annexed to comments along the lines of 'I was at school with…' or 'a friend of mine once worked with someone called…', mostly turn out to be fabrications. The names that follow are entirely genuine in that they have all been recorded in parish registers, birth, marriage and death records, census returns or other official documents. Whether some might be mistakes resulting from incorrect transcription is another issue, but one I have attempted to eliminate wherever possible. I should have liked to include Bennet Quicklay, for example, who married Dorathie [*sic*] Rotheram in Nottingham on 24 May 1592, but on closer inspection his surname turned out to be Quicksay, which is not as funny or erotically charged as a quick lay. I have chanced my arm with Kunt Rubbing – although his name may disappointingly turn out to be, as a serious genealogist has edited it, 'Knut Rebbing'.

Some names, of the ilk of Fanny and Gay, were not slang and did not possess an alternative meaning when they were conferred, but plenty of names have always meant the same thing, so it is extraordinary that they are so often encountered. Sometimes you come across 'golden doubles' – it's bad enough to be saddled with an unfortunate surname, but downright cruel if your parents then compound your problems by giving you an equally duff first name or names, as with Arse Arseson, Penis Fannie, Everhard Dick and Willy Penis. While you are pondering on this, visualize, if you can, the speeches at the Cock–Holder, Fuck–Knowls and Long–Dick weddings. Share in the horrible realization of many women who, through marriage, were destined to acquire some ghastly name, so that henceforth Ms Ramires was to be known as Mrs Arse or Ms Marten became Mrs Bollock – although, to be fair, there were probably just as many who were grateful to abandon such family names as Boobs, Anus or Bonk.

Once upon a time in America

Although the exclusively British names featured in *Potty, Fartwell & Knob* were a rich seam that had not previously been mined, in extending the quest globally, and in particular to the United States, a vast new repository of names has opened up. As well as early colonists, they include many immigrants. Emma Lazarus's poem, 'The New Colossus', inscribed on the Statue of Liberty, contains the lines, '"Give me your tired, your poor / Your huddled masses yearning to breathe free"', and so the United States attracted vast numbers of immigrants: in the period 1903–15 an average of 982,655 arrived every year. From 1892 to 1954 many of them arrived at Ellis Island and announced their names, which were promptly mangled by immigration officials or transliterated into an approximate English equivalent that was sometimes – although not as often as is sometimes stated – a deliberately ludicrous version. The records of passenger ship arrivals in New York and other ports have been particularly fruitful in revealing a range of bizarrely risqué names.

Beyond *Dances With Wolves*

A number of Native American names have also been included. Some readers may blanch at the apparent political incorrectness inherent in some of them, but such names were not imposed by outsiders. As anthropologists have discovered, many that sound pejorative were in fact coined by the tribal peoples themselves, whose descriptive skills and often considerable humour and inventiveness have resulted in a crop of truly remarkable and little-known names, as exemplified by John Big Crow who married Lucy Fast Bull Broken Leg in Todd, South Dakota, on 1 July 1921. There is also a refreshing lack of euphemism and obfuscation in Native American naming traditions: if someone's name was Dick and he had a broken nose, he would very likely be known as Dick Broken Nose (as, indeed, was a member of the Sioux tribe, born in 1897 and who served in the US Army in the First World War). It is perhaps worth noting, incidentally, that the popular belief that a baby would be named after the first thing its mother saw after childbirth is without foundation, so there is a regrettable absence of anyone called, as in the old joke, Two Dogs Fucking, but this omission is compensated for by several that are even ruder.

Names and slang

Some names contain elements of the specialized sexual slang that is rarely encountered beyond the realm of pornography. While admitting familiarity with them is tantamount to confessing to being an avid consumer of porn, they will be known to anyone with an interest in contemporary slang. If you are unacquainted with bukkake, felching, facials, strap-ons, fisting, teabagging and other erotic esoterica (which I had the task of explaining to my genteel editor), I recommend a good slang dictionary: *The New Partridge Dictionary of Slang and Unconventional English* (Oxford: Routledge, 2006) is expensive, but the best.

Fact or fiction?

By confining the entries to 'real' people, rather than the inventions of writers, many graphically named characters in books and on screen have sadly been set aside. You will not encounter Master Bates, as Dickens repeatedly refers to Charley Bates in *Oliver Twist*, Tosser, Gunman, the eponymous hero of a 1939 novel by Frank Carr or the shipmates of Captain Pugwash – Seaman Staines, Master Bates and Roger the cabin boy – which are an urban myth anyway. Nor will there be any delving into nominative determinism, the tendency of people to end up in professions that neatly match their names. There is nothing to suggest that Fanny Harlot, who shows up in Ore, Sussex, in the 1891 census, ever became a prostitute, but 'Fanny Harlot, The Whore from Ore' would have made for a great business card.

More Fuckers than Wankers

The sheer number of these names is amazing. In many instances, I have opted for a single example that particularly appealed to me, but I was often spoilt for choice where records list candidates running into the thousands.

But just how common are they? Although this makes no claim to be an exhaustive or precise statistical survey, an analysis of decennial US federal censuses (1790–1930), other censuses and voter lists and England censuses for the period 1841–1911 (plus some covering former British colonial dependencies, 1812–34) provides the following overview of the relative popularity of a fairly random selection of 'rude' surnames. This goes some way to counter claims that most such names must have resulted from transcription errors and that no one ever really bore them.

Surname	USA	UK	Total
Beaver	61,354	9,733	71,087
Cock	16,798	32,640	49,438
Balls	5,707	28,193	33,900
Fanny	7,564	21,409	28,973
Boner	18,212	1,408	19,620
Bonk	5,355	154	5,509
Bastard	313	2,891	3,204
Minge	2,519	162	2,681
Wank	2,562	86	2,648
Nipple	1,990	5	1,995
Fucker	1,697	88	1,785
Knob	1,709	76	1,785
Bollock	1,447	325	1,772
Boob	1,346	296	1,642
Sucker	1,178	434	1,612
Wanker	1,441	94	1,535
Cum	1,225	40	1,265
Prick	863	223	1,086
Bum	864	148	1,012
Bugger	897	49	946
Fart	764	103	867
Crap	524	85	609
Fuck	525	39	564
Anus	499	11	510

This is a theory that is undoubtedly true in occasional instances, but improbable when looking at the bigger picture as these names arise in official records on hundreds or thousands of occasions.

Surname	USA	UK	Total
Ass	390	18	408
Pussy	97	261	358
Slag	227	16	243
Penis	219	13	232
Shag	207	19	226
Tosser	198	20	218
Arse	182	5	187
Cunt	89	53	142
Tit	119	7	126
Anal	38	72	110
Shitter	77	29	106
Twat	16	58	74
Poof	65	4	69
Shagger	59	1	60
Pisser	52	4	56
Shit	51	5	56
Slut	36	18	54
Piss	43	7	50
Tits	36	1	37
Pube	31	2	33
Bumboy	25	0	25
Shitting	14	5	19
Pissing	17	0	17
Boobs	12	4	16

A declining asset

As I was concluding my research, Professor Richard Webber of King's College London published statistics that indicated that 'embarrassing' names were dwindling as more and more people changed them for innocuous alternatives. From the time of the 1881 census to 2008, he calculated, the number of people called 'Cock' had dwindled by 75 per cent, while 'Balls' had dropped by over 50 per cent. So it is apparent that as well as, I hope, providing a giggle or two, I am apparently recording a species of name that is already critically endangered and under threat of becoming extinct. It is as if a sort of natural selection is at work, filtering out the offbeat, the funny and the downright filthy names in favour of the more mundane.

Taking offence

It is a sad state of affairs, but the overarching reason for this decline is, of course, that some people find certain words offensive. The rude names in *Potty, Fartwell & Knob* were especially challenging. Some radio stations told me I couldn't say any of them on air, even if the programme was being pre-recorded and edited. Some censored those I could not say ('"Bum" is OK, but we'll have to ask the producer about "Willy"') while others even fretted over my saying the title of the book. But some people take offence very easily, while others – and that includes you, or you would not be reading this – acknowledge that they are just words, or, in the present context, names that many thousands have borne. That people received them from their parents or through marriage is an historical fact. Other than those who took the opportunity to change them, we must assume that they were perfectly happy with the names with which they were born or which they later acquired.

Whether or not such names should be changed is redolent of the old joke about the handsome and talented young actor who fails to get work because his name is Penis Van Lesbian. His agent pleads with him to change it, but pride in his family name runs deep and he repeatedly refuses, eventually parting company with the agent. Some years later the agent receives a fulsome letter from his former client explaining that after much soul-searching he finally accepted that he was right, and as a consequence of changing his name has found fame and fortune. He encloses a substantial cheque as an expression of his gratitude. You have probably beaten me to the punchline, but the letter is signed 'Dick Van Dyke'.

The bottom line is that we should not mock the Penis Van Lesbians of this world. On the contrary, in many instances these people have risen above whatever disability their names may have inflicted on them and emerged proud and strong from their experience. It is just that seen through others' eyes, like yours and mine, their names inspire an astonished and gently mirthful response. And what a struggle many of them must have had: just imagine being called Penis Hardon, Tess Tickle, Flamina Arsole, Jennie Talia, Anice Pair, Norma Stitz, Fucker Tucker or the more enigmatic Bonk Register or Wolf Porno.

Didn't they do well?

The 'Fartwell' in *Potty, Fartwell & Knob* was almost a celebration of a special ability, but the '…well' suffix applies in many other areas of endeavour in the following pages, hence we encounter individuals with such surnames as Arsewell, Cuntwell, Ballwell, Ballswell, Bedswell, Bumwell, Crapwell, Cockwell, Cockswell, Comewell, Dickswell, Dickwell, Fuckwell, Prickwell, Shagwell, Shitwell,

Suckwell and Wankwell. If anyone still bears such names, good luck to you and all your compatriots listed here.

X-tra features

While the personal names and the appropriate (or inappropriate, depending on how you view it) pairings form the core of the book, its range extends into other areas where rude names, whether accidental or deliberate, are encountered, among them those of film stars and bands, in rhyming slang and place names, domain names, acronyms and products. I hope you enjoy the journey – now fasten your seat belt.

Notes

Names are from the UK unless otherwise indicated.

'US census' refers to the decennial US census (1790–1930) unless otherwise noted.

Although years of birth taken from registrations are as recorded in the source, a birth late in a year may not have been registered until the following year. Ages are more commonly noted in census returns than years of birth, so the precise year of birth is *circa* and could be a year out either way.

Especially when infant mortality was high, baptisms usually followed soon after births. Baptisms were entered in the parish register, so the date and location, and often the names of both parents are known; the place of birth is generally not noted, but in most instances can be assumed was in the same locality.

Place of birth is noted where known, but it is either omitted or given at county level only in some sources, such as early censuses; 'np' means no place and 'nd' no date is indicated in the source.

The location of a registered birth is often the registration district – usually the nearest town with a register office – but not necessarily the exact place of birth, although these are recorded in census returns with either greater (down to parish level) or lesser ('London' or 'Dorset', for example) precision.

Gender is noted where it is not obvious from the name or context, but the sex of some is impossible to extrapolate from the available data.

The reasonable assumption has been made that short versions of some names would have been customarily used (Dick for Richard, Phil for Philip and so on). Some depend on a slight flight of imagination in pronunciation, hence 'Hugh' sounds awfully like 'huge' and combinations like 'Mike Hunt' sound like – well, you get the idea – though how else would you say names like 'Les Behan'? If you don't get them, try saying them out loud (ideally, in private).

Locations and county names are as they were at the time of the record – in some instances, places may now be in different counties: for example, Barnet moved from Hertfordshire (1837–51) to Middlesex (1852–1946) and back to Hertfordshire (1946–65) before becoming part of Greater London (1965–present); Wokingham was in Wiltshire until 1845, but is now in Berkshire. Readers may be surprised to see occasional Irish entries, but from 1801 to 1922 Ireland was part of the United Kingdom.

Russell Ash
Lewes, 2009
www.RussellAsh.com

GRAND TOUR – THE WORLD'S RUDEST NAMES

STARTING AT THE BOTTOM

'Bottom' names are a staple of British music hall comedy. It is hardly surprising, since we have so many of them: Lowbottom, Slipperbottom, Hughbottom, Rosebottom, Sidebottom, Winterbottom, Shoebottom, Rockbottom, Shipperbottom, Shovebottom, Fairbottom, Windbottom, Shufflebottom, Ramsbottom, Rawbottom, Highbottom, Glassbottom, Tarbottom, Rossbottom and Thickbottom, to name just twenty of them, not to mention all the Bottoms and Bottomleys. But, in the realm of extreme naming, 'bottom' is

pretty tame. What about 'arse' and 'anus' – has anyone ever been cursed with such names? Of course they have. Read on…

Jemima Allass
Born *c.*1861; died Barnsley, Yorkshire, 1893

Fanny Allbutt
Born Birmingham, Warwickshire, *c.*1864
(Birmingham, 1881 England census)

Ants Annus
Born 22 October 1924; died Warrington, Cheshire, May 1990

Able Anus
(Male) Born British Columbia, *c.*1888
(Sechelt, British Columbia, 1911 Canada census)
Able was the brother of Mary, Maggie and Augustina Anus.

Claude Anus
Born Saizerais, France, 4 April 1699

Hephzibah Ann Anus
Born City of London, 1850

Ivan Anus
Born Saskatchewan, British Columbia, 1905
(Vancouver, British Columbia, 1911 Canada census)

Joseph Frank Lay Anus
Resident of Inglewood, Maranoa, Queensland, 1919
(1901–36 Australian electoral rolls)

Maria Anus
Born Wesolygrond, Ortelsburg, Prussia, 22 August 1855

Peinus Anus
(Male) Born New York, *c.*1855 (New York, 1860 US census)

Phyllis Anus
Born Pennsylvania, *c.*1916 (Philadelphia, Pennsylvania, 1920 US census)

Urana Anus
(Female) Born Iowa, *c.*1872 (Winnebago, Iowa, 1880 US census)

Baleriana Arse
Married Juan Castelo, San José, Peru, 3 August 1891

Consepsion Arse
Married Rafael Bargas, La Inmaculada Concepción, Heredia, Costa Rica, 31 August 1842

Ecolastica Arse
Baptized Santa Lucia, Macari, Peru, 9 February 1886

Enelina Arse Arse
Baptized Purificación, Guachinango, Mexico, 18 May 1868

Geronimo Arse
Married Leona Ramires, La Inmaculada Concepción, Heredia, Costa Rica, 13 May 1860

Hugh Arse
Born Saint Mary Steps, Exeter, Devon, 1701

Although rare, Arse is recorded as a surname in sixteenth- and seventeenth-century England. Dorothy Arse, for example, the daughter of Francis Arse, was baptized in Barnstaple, Devon, on 18 April 1686. In the eighteenth century, a family of Arses, probably of Spanish origin and headed by José Ygnacio Arse, lived in Milton Bryan, Bedfordshire, but the British Arses appear to have died out or changed their names during the nineteenth century, the last recorded in any census being in 1881. They may perhaps have emigrated to the USA, where the Arses are much bigger and show up increasingly commonly (fifty-five of them in the 1930 US census), many of them immigrants mainly from Spanish-speaking countries.

Jesus Arse
Married Marta Chavarria, La Inmaculada Concepción,
Heredia, Costa Rica, 14 May 1829

Lupy Arse
(Female) Born Mexico, *c.*1862 (Gonzales, Texas, 1900 US census)
Lupy was the wife of Bentwrat Arse.

Maria Arse
Baptized San Pedro y San Pablo, Jilotepec de Abasolo,
Mexico, 30 December 1838

Presentasion Arse
Baptized San Bernardo, Tarija, Bolivia, 21 November 1850

Arse Arselicksen
Born Norway, *c.*1804 (Columbia, Wisconsin, 1850 US census)

Justin Arseman
Born Louisiana, *c.*1838 (Lafourche, Louisiana, 1860 US census)

Arse Arseson
Recorded in US General Land Office Records 1796–1907 as
owner of 79.78 acres in Iowa County, Wisconsin, 15 May 1857

Ursula Arsewell
Baptized Whaplode Drove, Lincolnshire, 5 June 1608

Anus Arslanyan
Born 5 March 1917; died Bexley, Kent, 2004

Flamina Arsole
Born Vitiana, Coreglia Antelminelli, Lucca, Italy, 6 October 1730

Harry Assel
Born Ohio, *c.*1885
(Cleveland Heights, Cuyahoga, Ohio, 1930 US census)

Dick Assman
Born Birmingham, Warwickshire, *c.*1797
(Lambeth, London, 1851 England census)

Hannah Aynus

Born North Walsham, Norfolk, *c.*1847
(Barnham Broom, Norfolk, 1861 England census)

Bad Ass

(Female) Born *c.*1888 (South Dakota, 1891 US Indian census)
Bad Ass was the sister of Smells Good.

Ivy Anal Baker

(Male – surprisingly) Born London, *c.*1906
(Edenbridge, Kent, 1911 England census)

Arsabella Bending

Born Payhembury, Devon, *c.*1818
(Feniton, Devon, 1851 England census)

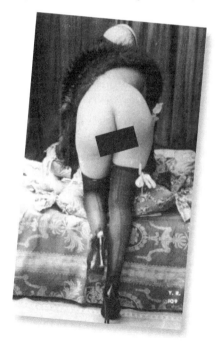

John Bigass
Born Detroit, Michigan, USA, 5 May 1887

March Booty
Born St Faiths, Norfolk, 1844

Harquless George Bootyman
Died Hull, Yorkshire, 1899

Elizabeth Pierce Bott
Born Liverpool, Lancashire, *c.*1848
(Liverpool, 1871 England census)

Arthur Henry Anulus Bottom
Baptized Sheffield, Yorkshire, 25 December 1859

Arthur Willie Bottom
Married Hannah M. Lockwood, Silkstone, Yorkshire, 26 July 1897

Fanny Bottom
Resident of Mullumbimby, Richmond, New South Wales, 1930
(1901–36 Australian electoral rolls)

Harry Bottom
Baptized Holy Trinity, Rugby, Warwickshire, 6 January 1861

Ellen Anal Brown
Born Birmingham, Warwickshire, *c.*1878
(Aston, Warwickshire, 1911 England census)

Fanny Bum
Born Oxfordshire, *c.*1839
(Binfield, Oxfordshire, 1841 England census)

Willy Bum
Born Derbyshire, *c.*1836
(Glossop, Derbyshire, 1861 England census)

Fanny Bumbot
Born St Pancras, London, *c.*1848
(Lambeth, London, 1871 England census)

Jane Bumcumlie
Born *c.*1816 (Huntingdon, 1841 England census)

Sarah Bumfit
Born Bradford, Yorkshire, *c.*1840 (Hipperholme-cum-Brighouse, Yorkshire, 1881 England census)

Dick Bumfitt
Born Chorlton, Lancashire, 1898

Arsfona Bumgardner
(Female) Born West Virginia, *c.*1885
(Williams, West Virginia, 1920 US census)

Randy Bumgardner
Born Ohio, USA, 9 July 1975; died 29 November 2004

Willy Bumgardner
Born Whicham, Cumberland, 18 October 1881

Willy Bumkum
Born Callington, Cornwall, *c.*1888
(Callington, 1891 England census)

Engelbert J. Bummer
Born Hull, Yorkshire, *c.*1847
(Holy Trinity, Yorkshire, 1871 England census)

Harry Bummy
Born Liverpool, Lancashire, *c.*1873
(West Derby, Lancashire, 1901 England census)

Arsie Bumpass
(Male) Born North Carolina, *c.*1915
(Allensville, North Carolina, 1920 US census)

Fanny Bumpass
Born Brackley, Buckinghamshire, 1842

Annus Bumphrey
(Female) Born Broomhill, Northumberland, *c.*1860
(Ashington, Northumberland, 1891 England census)

Isabella Bumup
Born Newcastle upon Tyne, Northumberland, *c.*1824 (Westgate, Northumberland, 1851 England census)

Annie Trollope Butt
Married Wandsworth, London, 1892

Bijou Butt
Born Okehampton, Devon, *c.*1860
(Gloucester, 1891 England census)

Fanny Butt
Born *c.*1902 (Barbour, Alabama, 1930 US census)

Harry Butt
Married Martha Maidment, Mere, Wiltshire, 26 April 1752

Messina Butt
Died Newton, Georgia, USA, 30 June 1924

Sexey Butt
Born Dundry, Somerset, *c.*1803
(Hanham, Gloucestershire, 1851 England census)

Seymour Butt
Born Bath, Somerset, 1875

Sarah Buttholes
Born Finchley, London, *c.*1876
(Willesden, London, 1891 England census)

Fanny Buttman
Born Grundisburgh, Suffolk, *c.*1880
(Burwash, Sussex, 1901 England census)

Moses Buttock
Born St Luke's, Middlesex, *c.*1827
(Deptford, London, 1881 England census)

Harry Butts
Born Muscatine, Iowa, USA, 28 June 1885

Scary Butts
(Male) Born Kentucky, *c.*1888
(Simpson, Kentucky, 1910 US census)

Seymour Butts
Born New York, 1894 (New York, 1900 US census)

Anal Cheek
(Male) Born Arkansas, *c.*1905 (Okemah, Oklahoma, 1920 US census)

Arsey Cubbin
(Female) Born Isle of Man, *c.*1868
(Braddan, Isle of Man, 1871 Isle of Man census)

Susanah Ashworth Anus De Boothfould
Buried Newchurch-in-Rossendale, Lancashire, 11 April 1723

Dogs Rectum
(Male) Born *c.*1870 (Idaho, 1897 US Indian census)

Jane Anus Elliott
Born Preston, Lancashire, *c.*1888 (Preston, 1911 England census)

Maria Entry
Born Maryland, *c.*1811 (New York, 1850 US census)

Fanny Fairbottom
Born Bridlington Quay, Yorkshire, *c.*1858
(Bridlington, 1861 England census)

Anus Fish
(Female) Born Iowa, *c.*1871
(Jefferson Woods, Oklahoma, 1920 US census)

Her Red Arse
Born *c.*1872 (South Dakota, 1893 US Indian census)

Asa Hole
Born Idaho, *c.*1898 (Spokane, Washington, 1910 US census)

William A. S. Hole
Born Burton upon Trent, Staffordshire, *c.*1887
(Buckhurst Hill, Essex, 1901 England census)

Hole In Bottom
(Male) Born *c.*1848 (Montana, 1890 US Indian census)

Hole In The Ass
(Female) Born *c.*1877 (Dakota Territory, 1886 US Indian census)

Augusta Hotass
Married Charles C. Morhart, Albemarle, Virginia,
USA, 7 September 1897

Mabel Hotbot
Born Québec, 22 June 1886
(Bonaventure, Québec, 1901 Canada census)

A. Hugass
Born Sweden, *c.*1905, crew on *City of New York*, Sweden–New York,
USA, arrived 25 April 1932

Anus Hughes
Died St Asaph, Denbighshire, 1847

Iron Bum Kelly
(Female) Born *c.*1883 (Nevada, 1904 US Indian census)

Hugh Janus
Born *c.*1898, passenger on *Doric*, Liverpool, England–Québec,
Canada, arrived 17 August 1926

Arundel Anus King
Born *c.*1847; died Wellington, Somerset, 1904

Anus Lane
Born Marylebone, London, 1879

Analella Longbottom
(Female) Born Yorkshire, *c.*1837
(Silsden, Yorkshire, 1861 England census)

Fanny Longbottom
Born Portsmouth, Hampshire
(Buttershaw, Yorkshire, 1891 England census)

Michael McAnus
Born Leigh, Lancashire, *c.*1892
(Chorlton-on-Medlock, Manchester, 1911 England census)

Joseph McArse
Born South Shields, Durham, 1917

Victoria McAss
Born Ontario, *c.*1888 (New Hamburg, Ontario, 1891 Canada census)

Anal McCranie
(Male) Born 1914 (Pondtown, Dodge, Georgia, 1930 US census)
Anal McCranie was the son of Reamer McCranie.

Mabel Anus Marshment
Born Camberwell, London, 1885

Anus Bibby May
Born Manchester, Lancashire, 1871

Isabella Mybum
Born Guernsey, Channel Islands, *c.*1834 (Ilminster, Somerset,
1851 England census)

Ann Nuss
Born Switzerland, *c.*1836 (Troy, Wisconsin, 1860 US census)

Harry A. Nuss
Born Ohio, *c.*1847 (Botkins, Shelby, Ohio, 1930 US census)

Arse Oats
(Female) Born Florida, 1898 (Walton, Florida, 1900 US census)

Charlotte Openbottom
Married Step Easley, Centenary Methodist Episcopal Church
South, Palestine, Anderson, Texas, USA, 27 July 1881

Maria Orifice
Born Feroleto Antico, Catanzaro, Calabria, Italy, 2 April 1797

Alice Pinckass
Married Perranarworthal, Cornwall, 29 September 1711

Anus Price
(Female) Born Missouri, 1870
(Tavern, Pulaski, Missouri, 1880 US census)

Anus C. Rapp
(Female) Born Indiana, 1887 (Chicago, Illinois, 1910 US census)

Mary Roughbottom
Baptized St Mary, Oldham, Lancashire, 17 January 1731

Anus Ruff
(Male) Born South Carolina, *c.*1875
(Heller, Newberry, South Carolina, 1920 US census)

Charlotte Booty Seamen
Born Thingoe, Suffolk, 1852

Jane Shagglebottom
Born Crewe, Cheshire, *c.*1880 (Crewe, 1911 England census)

Arse Silverhorn
(Female) Born Wisconsin, 1897
(Jefferson City, Wisconsin, 1900 US census)

Arson Skidmore
Married Gloucester, 1849

Sarah Smallass
Married John Watson, Tivetshall St Mary, Norfolk, 21 May 1751

Sold His Ass
(Male) Born *c*.1854 (Dakota Territory, 1887 US Indian census)

R. Sole
Baptized St Martin-in-the-Fields, London, 5 August 1582

R. Soles
(Male) Born Greenwich, London, 1844

Uranus Sparks
Born 13 July 1921; married Macon, Alabama, USA,
August 1956; died 1 December 1990

Mary A. Stripperbottom
Born Bolton, Lancashire, *c*.1834
(Tonge with Haulge, Lancashire, 1891 England census)

Arsley Swell
Baptized St Martin-in-the-Fields, London, 7 July 1745

Arsena Titus
Born New York, *c*.1826
(Hamburg, Erie, New York, 1850 US census)

Alice Winkbottom
Born Clifton, Lancashire, *c*.1871 (Clifton, 1891 England census)

Enema Bottomley Wood
Died Huddersfield, Yorkshire, 1904

Mary Zarse
Born Cornwall, *c*.1811
(Mevagissey, Cornwall, 1841 England census)

A LOAD OF COCK AND BALL

As well as individuals bearing these surnames in censuses, a curiously precise 17,000 births of baby Balls were registered in England in the period 1837–2005, along with a profusion of Cocks (15,792) and the rarer Pricks (57) and Bollocks (35). As with related names and those of their female counterparts, they seem destined to go the way of other 'embarrassing' names as their bearers steadily concede defeat in the battle between valiantly preserving the family name and putting up with the baggage that goes with it, or changing it.

Gonads Anchondo
Born Mexico, *c.*1897 (El Paso, Texas, 1920 US census)

John Thomas Badcock
Baptized Great Bowden, Leicestershire, 18 June 1868

Low John Baldcock
Born Spalding, Lincolnshire, 1840

Ellis Poo Ball
Born Leeds, Yorkshire, 1842

George Slack Ball
Born Nottingham, 1847

Harold Tickle Ball
Born Tavistock, Devon, 20 July 1909

Lackary Ball
Born Coleshill, Hertfordshire, *c.*1808
(Amersham, Buckinghamshire, 1871 England census)

William Loose Ball
Married Holsworthy, Cornwall, 1888

Marais Ballaxe
Betrothed to Sara Bloch
(2 August 1884 Paris, France marriage banns)

Bessie Ballhatchet
Born *c.*1860; died Plymouth, Devon, 1918

Benjamin Balls Balls
Born Newmarket, Cambridgeshire, 1875

Claude Balls
Born Texas, *c.*1908 (Houston, Texas, 1930 US census)

Golden Balls
Baptized Aylsham, Norfolk, 26 September 1813
His son was also called Golden Balls.

Harry Balls
Married Thingoe, Suffolk, 1869

Horatio Finer Balls Balls
Born St Luke, London, 1842

John Mean Balls
Died Blything, Suffolk, 1869

Max Balls
Born New York, *c.*1893 (New York, 1930 US census)

Minnie Balls
Born West Ham, Essex, 1870

Nora Balls
Born Cratfield, Suffolk, *c.*1809 (Cratfield, 1891 England census)

Pinkie Balls
Died Milam, Texas, USA, 31 December 1917

Violet Minnie Balls
Born St Pancras, London, 1896

Willy Hugh Balls
Born Kensington, London, 1874

Minnie Ballsacker
Recorded as mother of Ethel Louisa Brinkmeyer, born St Louis,
Missouri, USA, 3 August 1908

Harry Balz
Born Maryland, *c.*1865 (Baltimore, Maryland, 1870 US census)

Dick Barecock
Baptized Stagsden, Bedfordshire, 29 August 1790

Dick Bellend
Baptized St Mary Magdalene,
Bermondsey, London, 6 February 1848

Connie Bellendin
Born Strood, Kent, *c.*1891
(Lambeth, London, 1911 England census)

Willy Bicardick
Baptized Franham, Yorkshire, 10 July 1576

Xpofer Bickerdick
Married Martha Hunt, North Luffenham, Rutland, 15 May 1600

Big Dick
Born *c.*1860 (Mojave, Arizona, 1902 US Indian census)

John Bigone
Born California, *c.*1913 (San Francisco,
California, 1920 US census)

It is uncertain whether his surname was pronounced as 'Big one'.

Dick Bigrigg
Born Gateshead, Durham, 1893

Big Tool
Born *c.*1826 (Montana, 1891 US Indian census)

Willie Bigun
Born Massachusetts, *c.*1871
(New Ashford, Massachusetts, 1880 US census)

Angles Bollock
(Female) Married Scioto, Ohio, USA, 21 July 1881

Arthur Bollock
Born Hull, Yorkshire, *c.*1896
(Grimsby, Lincolnshire, 1911 England census)

Asse Bollock
(Male) Born North Carolina, *c.*1850
(Pactolus, Pitt, North Carolina, 1880 US census)

Basha Bollock
(Female) Born North Carolina, *c.*1849
(Pactolus, Pitt, North Carolina, 1880 US census)

Dick Bollock
Married Dorathy [*sic*] Marten, St Mabyn, Cornwall, 16 June 1659

Fanny Bollock
Born Battersea, London, *c.*1850 (Battersea, 1851 England census)

Hugh Bollock
Born New York, *c.*1877 (Brooklyn, New York, 1880 US census)

Max Bollock
Born New York, *c.*1904 (Brooklyn, New York, 1910 US census)

Minnie Bollock
Born 15 January 1896; died Saint Paul, Minnesota, USA, May 1986

Urinson Bollock
(Male) Born Iowa, *c.*1878 (Rippey, Greene, Iowa, 1880 US census)

Willy Bollock
Resident of Maffra, Gippsland, Victoria, 1914
(1901–36 Australian electoral rolls)

Jane Bollocks
Born Scotland, *c.*1840
(St Werburgh, Derbyshire, 1871 England census)

William Bollocks
Married Anne Hodges, Withington, Herefordshire,
13 November 1574

Dick Boner
Born Indiana, *c.*1910 (Allen, Indiana, 1920 US census)

Penis Broadaway
Born Anson, North Carolina, USA, 15 February 1917

Jane Cock Burgers
Born Camborne, Cornwall, *c.*1817 (Camborne, 1861 England census)

Dick Butter
Born Virginia, *c.*1865 (Salem, Virginia, 1930 US census)

Minnie Castrator
Born Collingwood, Ontario, Canada, 24 April 1872

Orange Castrator
Born Wisconsin, *c.*1866 (Moniteau, Missouri, 1870 US census)

Dick Cheese
Born Georgia, 1867 (Nance, Georgia,1900 US census)

Fanny Cleaver
Born Missouri, *c.*1870 (Lake, Indiana, 1910 US census)
A 'fanny cleaver' is a slang term for a large penis.

Analese Cock
Born Burnley, Lancashire, 1859

Dick Willy Cock
Plymouth, Devon, 1853
His name is a rare example of a penile triple.

E. Love Cock
(Male) Born St Pancras, London, *c.*1869
(Shoreditch, London, 1901 England census)

Everard Cock
Born Wells, Somerset, 1890

George Alfred Pink Cock
Born Shoreditch, London, 1852

George Asbery Hard Cock
Born 18 May 1884
(Jackson, Tennessee, USA, First World War draft registration)

Ida Cock
Married Jean Baptiste Paul Paquet, Paris, France, 22 September 1901
Ida Cock was the daughter of Philomene Boobs.

Iva Cock

(Female) Born Illinois, *c.*1869
(South English, Keokuk, Iowa, USA, 1925 Iowa state census)

John Thomas Cock

Born *c.*1859; died Penzance, Cornwall, 1894
*He was one of at least forty-six John Thomas Cocks born in
England and Wales in the period 1837–1983.*

Joseph Long Cock

Born Mevagissey, Cornwall, *c.*1863
(Mevagissey, 1871 England census)

Long Cock

Born *c.*1873; passenger on *Eastern*, Canton,
China–Melbourne–Sydney, Australia, arrived 2 July 1901

Lovely Cock

(Female) Born Cornwall, *c.*1781
(Mylor, Cornwall, 1841 England census)

Minnie Cock

Born Nova Scotia, 24 December 1877
(Colchester, Nova Scotia, 1901 Canada census)

Norman Sawyer Cock

Born Paddington, London, 1898

Ophelia Cock

Born New York, *c.*1860 (New York, 1870 US census)

Pink Cock

(Male) Born Texas, *c.*1870 (Harrison, Texas, 1880 US census)

Prince Cock

(Female) Born Texas, *c.*1873 (Weatherford, Texas, 1880 US census)

Tinie Cock

Born Pembroke, 1861

Violet Cock

Resident of Parramatta, New South Wales, 1930
(1901–36 Australian electoral rolls)

William Curling Cock
Born Dover, Kent, 1861

Woodman Cock
Born Roche, Cornwall, *c*.1856
(Burney, Cornwall, 1871 England census)

Rose Cockhead
Born Bladon, Oxfordshire, *c*.1874
(Begbroke, Oxfordshire, 1901 England census)

Ophelia Cocks
Born Oxfordshire, *c*.1800
(St Marylebone, London, 1871 England census)

Bellend Cokella
(Female) Born Ireland, *c*.1840
(Tottington Lower End, Lancashire, 1871 England census)

Tosibio Cojones
Father of Flerntina Cojones, married Alfonso Chavez, Tabaco,
Philippines, 25 September 1950
'Cojones' is Spanish for 'balls' – but I am sure you knew that.

Covering Of A Mans Peenis [*sic*]
(aka Pah Sha Cunt)
(Male) Born *c*.1846 (Idaho, 1887 US Indian census)

Dick Cream
Born Diptford, Devon, *c*.1833
(Staverton, Devon, 1851 England census)

Crooked Prick
(Male) Born *c*.1868 (South Dakota, 1887 US Indian census)

Earnest Crotch
Born Norwich, Norfolk, *c*.1879
(Bowling, Yorkshire, 1891 England census)

Penis Curling
(Male) Born Southall, Middlesex, *c*.1903
(Uxbridge, Middlesex, 1911 England census)

Dick Dangle
Born c.1925 (Logan, Nebraska, 1930 US census)

Willie Dangle
Born Pennsylvania, 1887 (Eldred, Pennsylvania, 1900 US census)

Harry Danglers
Born New Jersey, c.1900
(Guantánamo Bay, Cuba, 1920 US census)

José Desiré De Cock
Married Kensington, London, 1897

Anita Dick
Born c.1918 (Ellinwood, Kansas, 1930 US census)

Effing Dick
(Male) Born Glasgow, Lanarkshire, c.1848
(Glasgow, 1861 Scotland census)

Elephant Dick
(Male) Born Nevada, c.1870 (Queen, Nevada, 1920 US census)

Everhard Dick
Born Germany, 28 December 1903
(23 October 1931 application for US naturalization)

Hugh Dick
Born Sheffield, Yorkshire, 1904

Ima Dick
Born Missouri, c.1889 (Johnson, Oklahoma, 1920 US census)

Iona Dick
Born Ontario, 1888
(Saltcoats, Saskatchewan, 1911 Canada census)

Little Dick
Born Northroad, Cheshire, c.1851
(Wolstanton, Staffordshire, 1881 England census)

Long Dick
Born California, c.1865 (Alpine, California, 1910 US census)

Lotta Dick
Born France, *c.*1829 (Saint Louis, Missouri, 1880 US census)

Robert Lock Hard Dick
Born Philadelphia, Pennsylvania, USA, 26 December 1892
(Delaware, Pennsylvania, Second World War draft registration)

Willie Manhood Dickerson
Born King's Lynn, Norfolk, 1864

Odd Dicks
Died Thrapston, Northamptonshire, 1886

Harry Dong
Born Birmingham, Warwickshire, *c.*1847 (Edgbaston,
Warwickshire, 1861 England census)

John Thomas Dong
Born Bradford, Yorkshire, *c.*1868 (Bradford, 1901 England census)

Long Dong
Born China, *c.*1887 (Spokane, Washington, 1930 US census)

Darling Donger
Born Muston, Leicestershire, *c.*1899 (Muston, 1901 England census)

Jenny Ball Donger
Born King's Lynn, Norfolk, 1889

Willy Droop
Resident of Kennedy, Queensland, 1905
(1901–36 Australian electoral rolls)

Willy Durex
Born Indiana, *c.*1880 (Louisville, Kentucky, 1880 US census)
Non-Brits may wish to know that Durex is the bestselling brand
of condom in the UK. People from Australia, where Durex is a
type of sticky tape, are often as confused by this as Britons are
when they attempt to buy condoms down under.

Dick End
Married Sarah Hunt, Lacock, Wiltshire, 21 July 1755

Arnold Eunuch
Married Ann Mabie, Sherburn-in-Elmet, Yorkshire,
25 January 1701

Dick Everhard
Married Frances Lee, Billesley, Warwickshire, 11 September 1653

Penis Fannie
(Female) Born North Carolina, *c.*1874
(Buncombe, North Carolina, 1910 US census)

Bollock Fisher
Born Ohio, 1900 (Cleveland City, Cuyahoga, Ohio, 1900 US census)

Fish Prick
(Male) Born *c.*1864 (Montana, 1887 US Indian census)

Elwood Foreskin
Born *c.*1920 (South Huntingdon, Westmoreland, Pennsylvania, 1930 US census)

Fore Skin
(Male) Born *c.*1800 (Idaho, 1890 US Indian census)

Four Balls
(Male) Born *c.*1842 (Montana, 1891 US Indian census)

Frozen Pecker
(Female) Born *c.*1824 (Dakota Territory, 1889 US Indian census)

Willy Galore
Born California, *c.*1894 (San Bruno, California, 1920 US census)

Willy Prick Gibbs
Born Surrey, *c.*1833 (Worplesdon, Surrey, 1871 England census)

Floyd Penis Goff
Son of Joseph H. Goff and Nancy Virginia Buzzard, born 23 June 1867; died Lawford, Ritchie, West Virginia, USA, 29 October 1931

Josiah Gonad
Born Roborough, Devon, *c.*1833
(Mile End, London, 1891 England census)

Augustas [*sic*] Gonads
Born Mexico, *c.*1896 (Cameron, Texas, 1930 US census)

Selina Goolie
Born Bromfield, Shropshire, c.1863
(Malvern, Worcestershire, 1901 England census)
'Goolie', meaning testicle, comes from the Hindi 'gooli', a pellet.
The term was originally adopted by British military personnel.

Philapena Griesedick
Born Hesse-Kassel, Prussia, c.1838
(St Louis, Missouri, 1860 US census)

Mealota Hardcock
Born Norfolk, c.1832 (Spotland, Lancashire, 1861 England census)

Dickson Head
Born Pennsylvania, 1892
(South Fayette, Pennsylvania, 1900 US census)

Dick Helmet
Born Russia, c.1898; passenger on *Prinz Friedrich Wilhelm*, Bremen,
Germany–New York, USA, arrived 8 May 1911

Charles Penis Horn
Married St George, Hanover Square, London, 1845

Harrold [*sic*] Horney
Born Nebraska, 1896 (Tobias Village, Nebraska, 1900 US census)

Will Hung
Born *c.*1875 (Helena, Arkansas, 1900 US census)

Well Hung
Born Texas, *c.*1867 (Harris, Texas, 1920 US census)

Wellman Hung
Born Michigan, *c.*1896 (Detroit, Michigan, 1900 US census)

Penis King
(Female) Born North Carolina, *c.*1907
(Greenville, North Carolina, 1910 US census)
Penis was the daughter of Willy and Lovie King.

Sidney Herbert Knacker
Baptized St Mary the Virgin, Dover, Kent, 13 January 1803

Bob Knob
Born New York, *c.*1823 (Elmira, New York, 1860 US census)

Fat Kock
Born Hong Kong, *c.*1889, crew on *Colusa*,
Hong Kong–San Francisco, California, USA, arrived 18 July 1913

Dick Lingam
Born Massachusetts, *c.*1864 (Chicago, Illinois, 1930 US census)
A lingam is the male counterpart of the female yoni.

Organ B. Long
Married Jennie Pruett, Dekalb, Alabama, USA, 22 December 1893

Willy Long
(Female) Born Luton, Bedfordshire, *c.*1896
(Luton, 1901 England census)

V. Longcock
(Male) Born *c.*1876; passenger on *Lake Winnipeg*, Québec,
Canada–Liverpool, England, arrived October 1897

Ada McBollock
Born Birmingham, Warwickshire, *c*.1881
(Birmingham, 1881 England census)

Willy McCock
Married Jean Harper, St Cuthbert's, Edinburgh,
Midlothian, 21 December 1760

Laurence McPenis
Born Ireland, *c*.1842 (Washington, Indiana, 1870 US census)

Dick Manhood
Baptized Glemsford, Suffolk, 17 May 1657

Mashing Prick
(Male) Born *c*.1883 (South Dakota, 1887 US Indian census)

Carie Mycock
Born Saskatchewan, *c*.1909 (Regina, Saskatchewan, Canada, 1916
Manitoba, Saskatchewan and Alberta census)

Pat Mycock
Born Burton upon Trent, Staffordshire, 1927

John Nadger
Married Elizabeth Lund, Plumpton, Lancashire, 31 January 1704

Christian Nicewanger
Born Indiana, *c*.1871 (Harrison City, Indiana, 1880 US census)

Harriet Nicewonger
Born Ilkeston, Derbyshire, *c*.1876 (Ilkeston, 1891 England census)

Olney W. Nicewonger
Born Pennsylvania, *c*.1880
(Salem, Forsyth, North Carolina, 1900 US census)

Ole P. Niss
Born 1897; passenger on *Eclipse*, Esperanza, British Columbia,
Canada–Seattle, Washington, USA, arrived 2 February 1946

Peter P. Niss
Born Norway, 1865 (Cairo, Minnesota, 1900 US census)

No Balls
(Male) Born *c.*1868 (Fort Peck, Montana, 1886 US Indian census)

Dick Nothard
Born Sculcoates, Yorkshire, 1853

Christopher Nuts
Born Birmingham, Warwickshire, *c.*1860
(Birmingham, 1891 England census)

Hugh Organ
Born Ireland, *c.*1839 (Gaines, New York, 1860 US census)

Miles O'Toole
Born *c.*1839; died St Pancras, London, 1866

Chris Peacock
Born Askrigg, Yorkshire, 1837

Drew Peacock
Born North Carolina, 1870
(Wilson, North Carolina, 1900 US census)

Claude Pecker
Born Atcham, Shropshire, 1897

Dick Pecker
Married Hannah Gibbs, Spitalfields Christ Church, Stepney,
London, 2 September 1753

Boney Penile
Born North Carolina, USA, 6 October 1881;
died 6 September 1954

Elizabeth Penile
Daughter of James Penile, baptized Bishop Norton,
Lincolnshire, 7 March 1627

Ambrosia Penis
Born Kentucky, *c.*1858 (Macon, Missouri, 1860 US census)

Jesus Penis
Born Puerta Del Refugio, San Luis Potosi, Mexico, 3 April 1858;
died 12 October 1895

Manuel Penis
Born Spain, *c.*1893; passenger on *Metapan*, Kingston,
Jamaica–New York, USA, arrived 17 May 1923

Minnie Penis
Born Mississippi, 1892 (Tate, Mississippi, 1900 US census)

Peter Penis
Married Experance [*sic*] Porige, Yarmouth, Massachusetts,
America, 2 February 1734

Pinkey Penis
(Female) Born Mississippi, *c.*1870
(Tate, Mississippi, 1900 US census)

Raghed Penis
(Female) Married Joseph Mithers, Ripley, Missouri,
USA, 20 March 1880

Willy Penis
Born 1842 (Brushy Mountain Township, Wilkes,
North Carolina, 1900 US census)

Harry Chopper J. Percy
Born Gravesend, Kent, 1879

Cyril Twocock Peters
Born Gravesend, Kent, 1906

Willy Pinkstaff
Born Lawrence, Illinois, USA, 6 August 1841

Dick Plonker
Baptized Alverstoke, Hampshire,
11 December 1586

Dick Prick
Born *c.*1790; died Machynlleth,
Powys, 1870

Hugh Prick
Born Shropshire, *c.*1801
(Oswestry, Shropshire, 1851
England census)

Misericordia Prick
Married Susanna Land,
Stansfield, Suffolk, 4 July 1731

Hugh Penis Pritchard
Born 1915; died Caernarfon,
Gwynedd, 1990

Dick Putz
Born Michigan, *c.*1910 (Wayne, Michigan, 1910 US census)
Yiddish has many synonyms for the penis, including shmuck,
schlong *or* shlong, shmeckel *and* shvanz. Putz *rose to
attention following its appearance in Philip Roth's seminal work,*
Portnoy's Complaint *(1969).*

Dick Rampant
Father of Mary Rampant, baptized Dorking,
Surrey, 21 February 1713

Penis Rough
Born Ireland, *c.*1831 (Liverpool, Lancashire, 1871 England census)

Harry Sack
Born Russia, *c.*1885 (Spotswood, New Jersey, 1920 US census)

Circumcision Sanchez
Born Spain, *c.*1902 (Youngstown, Ohio, 1930 US census)

Adolph Schlong
Born Bavaria, *c.*1864 (Philadelphia, Pennsylvania, 1880 US census)
*Adolph Schlong was recorded in the 1880 census as the
nephew of Mary Fister.*

Harry Schlong
Born New York, *c.*1877 (New York, 1910 US census)

Dick Shaft
Born Littleover, Derbyshire, *c.*1883
(Derby, 1901 England census)

Dick Shaver
Born Alabama, *c.*1817 (Montgomery, Alabama, 1870 US census)

Hugh Shmuck
Born Germany, *c.*1864 (Toledo, Ohio, 1910 US census)

Willie Shortcock
Born Georgia, *c.*1895 (Fulton, Georgia, 1920 US census)

Shot To Penis
Born *c.*1843 (Dakota Territory, 1886 US Indian census)

Shows His Cock
Born *c.*1830 (Montana, 1887 US Indian census)

Skins His Penis
Born *c.*1867 (Dakota Territory, 1886 US Indian census)

Willy Smallball
Born Ireland, *c.*1832
(Kingston upon Thames, Surrey, 1881 England census)

Dick Surprise
Born Cheshire, *c.*1822 (Chester, Cheshire, 1851 England census)

Willy Surprise
Born Ireland, *c.*1841
(Alverstoke, Hampshire, 1871 England census)

Dick Swinger
Born Switzerland, *c.*1842 (Stewart, Tennessee, 1870 US census)

Amelia Testes
Born Kent, *c.*1857 (Kensington, London, 1881 England census)

Thomas Testes
Born *c.*1850 (Washington, Virginia, 1910 US census)

Testicle Head
(Male) Born *c.*1870 (Dakota
Territory, 1886 US Indian census)

Tess Tickle
Born Little Rock, Arkansas, USA, *c.*1893; married John H. Tickle;
died Fort McPherson, Fulton, Georgia, USA, 29 December 1923

John Todger
Born Gringham, Dorset, *c.*1825
(Weston-super-Mare, Somerset, 1891 England census)

Hugh Tool
Born Ireland, *c.*1830 (La Salle, Illinois, 1880 US census)

Willy Treblecock
Born St Marylebone, London, 1850

Eunuch Trusty
Born Illinois, *c.*1834 (Chickasaw, Iowa, 1860 US census)

Peter Twoballs
Born Wyoming, *c.*1852 (Rosebud, Montana, 1910 US census)

James Twococks
Born Bermondsey, London, 1861

Dick Upright
Married Exeter, Devon, 1893

Thomas Adolphus Treblecock Vincent
Resident of Kooyong, Victoria, 1909
(1901–36 Australian electoral rolls)

Penis Walkawitz
Born Russia, 1859
(Hot Springs City, Garland, Arkansas, 1900 US census)

Hugh Wang
Married California, USA, 1962

Washing Prick
(Female) Born *c.*1862 (South Dakota, 1887 US Indian census)

Hampton Wick
Born South Carolina, *c.*1819
(Union, South Carolina, 1860 US census)
*Hampton Wick is the London suburb that gave rise to the
rhyming slang, Hampton Wick = prick. Mr Wick is a rare
example of a person bearing this name.*

Stinkie Wiley
Born South Carolina, *c.*1898 (Chatham, Georgia, 1910 US census)

John Thomas Willy
Baptized St George the Martyr, Southwark,
London, 25 December 1812

Willy Willy
Born Ireland, *c.*1844 (Kensington, London, 1851 England census)

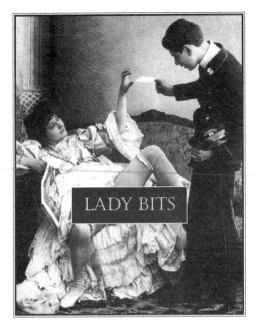

LADY BITS

Historically, the 'C-word' and its variants crop up as both a first name and surname in Britain. There was a Simon Sitbithe-cunte recorded in Norfolk in 1167 in a pipe roll (a financial record), John Fillecunt in a Lancashire assize roll of 1246, Robert Clevecunt in a Yorkshire subsidy roll of 1302 and Bele Wydecunthe in a Norfolk subsidy roll of 1328. The discovery of Fanny Cunt and her family in the 1881 England census launched a debate as to whether anyone really ever bore such a surname, related name or synonym. The answer, to those who doubt it, appears to be that plenty did, although it is also apparent that such names have dwindled in numbers along with other 'embarrassing' related names. The 1911 England census has so far produced only a pair of Cunts.

Charles Acunt

Born Switzerland, c.1883; passenger on *Olympic*, Southampton,
England–New York, USA, arrived 17 January 1923

Cunt Ah

Born China, c.1842 (Stanislaus, California, 1860 US census)

Mary Allcunt

Born Demerara, British Guiana, c.1815
(Chelsea, London, 1881 England census)

Cunts Goston de Arschot

Born c.1849; passenger on *Normandie*, Le Havre,
France–New York, USA, arrived 3 August 1885

Fanny Barer

Born Ireland, c.1842; passenger on *Victory*, Liverpool,
England–New York, USA, arrived 23 December 1862

Anita Beaver

Born Wisconsin, c.1904 (Granton, Wisconsin, 1920 US census)

Fanny Beaver

Born Bourne, Lincolnshire, 1839

Harry Beaver

Baptized St Mary's, Portsea, Hampshire, 21 November 1812

Love Beaver

(Male) Born North Carolina, c.1903
(China Grove, Rowan, North Carolina, 1920 US census)

Pinkie Beaver

Born c.1897 (Unicoi, Tennessee, 1930 US census)

Randy Beaver

(Female) Born Pennsylvania, c.1897
(Middle Smithfield, Pennsylvania, 1910 US census)

Beaver That Stretches

(Female) Born c.1848 (Montana, 1893 US Indian census)

Cunt Berger

Born Germany, c.1878 (Sunderland, Durham, 1901 England census)

Cunt Stubbee Billy
Private in Major Blue's detachment
(Indiana, America, War of 1812 service records)

Phoebe Cream Box
Born *c.*1826; died Manchester 1887
She was not the only Manchester-based Phoebe Cream Box –
another was born in 1889.

Clit Bush
Died Jackson, Georgia, USA, 14 November 1951

Curley Bush
(Male) Born Aldeburgh, Suffolk, *c.*1841
(Aldeburgh, 1851 England census)

Fanny Bush
Married Francis Cox, Ringwood, Hampshire, 7 February 1824

Ginger Bush
Born Pemberton Township, Burlington, New Jersey,
USA, 12 July 1861

Bush Clit
Born *c.*1890 (Jackson, Georgia, 1920 US census)

Cafe Clito
Born Oregon, USA, 16 April 1897; died April 1963

Jean Conneau
Born Belgium, *c.*1876 (Bloomsbury, London, 1901 census)
Another man with the same name, French naval officer and air
racing pilot Jean Conneau (1880–1937), used the nom d'air
André Beaumont, *partly to get round a rule that navy pilots*
could not take part in races, but also because in French his
surname is a synonym for 'cunt'. The related word, 'connerie',
meaning nonsense or bollocks, amuses French cineastes
whenever Sean Connery is on the bill.

Cow Cunt
(Male) Born *c.*1817 (Fort Peck, Montana, 1887 US Indian census)

Fanny Crack
Born Barrow, Suffolk, *c*.1848 (Kingsbury, Middlesex, 1871 census)

Fanny Cream
Married Robert Hardy, Eaton Socon, Bedfordshire, 13 August 1798

Fanny Crevice
Baptized Old Swinford, Worcestershire, 16 September 1838

Charlotte Crotch
Born Norwich, Norfolk, 1846

Cum Muff
(Female) Born *c*.1868 (Utah, 1887 US Indian census)

A. Cunt
(Female) Baptized St James, Colchester, Essex, 1 March 1684

Ann Cunt
Baptized Seend, Wiltshire, 25 October 1767

Emma Cunt
Born *c*.1845 (Philadelphia, 1870 US census)

Fannie Cunt
Born North Carolina, *c*.1852 (Washington, Texas, 1870 US census)

Fanny Cunt
Born Colchester, Essex, *c*.1839
(Hastings, Sussex, 1891 England census)

Fanny Cunt lived at 3 Eversfield Place, Hastings, with a family of Cunts: her son Alfred Cunt, born in New Zealand, and her son Richard 'Dick' Cunt and her daughters Ella and Violet Cunt, all of whom were born in Cape Colony (South Africa). Fanny is described as 'living on her own means', having presumably acquired her unfortunate surname through marriage and returned from the colonies with her four children, but apparently minus Mr Cunt. A local campaigner recently attempted unsuccessfully to have a commemorative plaque erected to her memory on the kebab house that today operates at her former address.

Ida Cunt
Married John L. Peterson, Laporte, Indiana, USA,
31 October 1895

Ransom Cunt
Born South Carolina, *c.*1815
(South Carolina, 1870 US census)

Sarah Cunt
Born Walcot, Lincolnshire, *c.*1856
(Grantham, Lincolnshire, 1911 England census)

Willie Cunt
Born London, England, *c.*1874; died Waterloo, Ontario,
Canada, 24 December 1881

Rose Cunte
Born Canada, *c.*1876 (Cleveland, Ohio, 1920 US census)

Ruby Cunte
Born *c.*1908 (Dawson, Texas, 1930 US census)

Santa Cunte
(Female) Born Italy, *c.*1844
(San Justo, Santa Fe, Argentina, 1895 Argentina census)

Cunt Get Up
(Female) Born *c.*1836 (Montana, 1895 US Indian census)

Worthy Cuntilla
Born Broughton, Wiltshire, *c.*1825
(Walcot, Somerset, 1861 England census)

Constant Cunting
Born 5 May 1946; died Arizona, USA, 1 June 2004

Christian Cuntlay
(Female) Born Ellon, Aberdeenshire, *c.*1835
(Cruden, Aberdeenshire, 1871 Scotland census)

James Cunts
Baptized Bank Street Unitarian Church, Bolton-le-Moors,
Lancashire, 28 May 1757

George Cuntsman
Born Illinois, *c.*1862 (Carlinville, Illinois, 1880 US census)

Elizabeth Cuntwell
Married Frank J. Boelm, Bartholemew County, Indiana,
USA, 5 August 1884

Dick Cunty
Born *c.*1843; died Charleston, South Carolina, USA, 5 July 1881

Honore Cunty
Born *c.*1823; passenger on *Martin Luther,* arrived
Australia 9 February 1842

Matilda Cunty
Born Truro, Cornwall, *c.*1839
(St Austell, Cornwall, 1911 England census)
*At the time of the 1911 census, the Cunty household consisted of
Matilda and her two sons, Arthur Cunty and Thomas Cunty, both
blacksmiths, and her grandson, Edwin Phillips – who had
mercifully escaped the family surname.*

Pricy Cunty
Born West Virginia, *c.*1867 (Logan, West Virginia, 1920 US census)

O. L. Cuntz
Born USA, *c.*1831; passenger on *La Champagne,* Le Havre,
France–New York, USA, arrived 3 February 1891

Annie Fagina
Born Austria, *c.*1872 (Chicago, Illinois, 1910 US census)
*Her name is prophetically close to that of Alotta Fagina, the Pussy
Galore spoof played by Fabiana Udenio in the film* Austin
Powers: International Man of Mystery *(1997).*

Furry Fannie
Born 14 August 1915; died New Derry, Pennsylvania,
USA, 14 March 2000

Labia Fannie
(Male) Born Indiana, *c.*1883
(San Bernardino, California, 1900 US census)

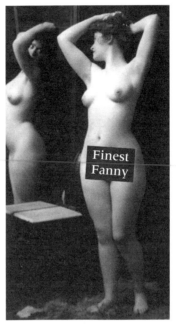

Finest
Fanny

Married Berrie Vista, New Madrid, Missouri, USA,
18 January 1911

Hugh Fanny
Born Staffordshire, *c.*1839
(Wolverhampton, Staffordshire, 1841 England census)

Iva Fanny
(Female) Born *c.*1915
(Pungoteague, Accomack, Virginia, 1930 US census)

Jenny Talia Ferro
Born Virginia, *c.*1857 (Massies, Nelson, Virginia, 1880 US census)

Fanny Flasher
Married Victor Grenbaum, Humberside, Lincolnshire, 1920

Pinkus Gash
(Male) Born Russia, *c.*1888
(Spitalfields, London, 1891 England census)
Pinkus was the son of Fanny and Isaac Gash.

Alfred Cunt Gee
Born Eynsford, Kent, *c.*1903 (Eynsford, 1911 England census)

Vagina Glasscock
Born Alabama, *c.*1889
(Somerville, Morgan, Alabama, 1910 US census)

Beaver Goodykoontz
Born California, USA, 14 October 1894; died Los Angeles,
California, USA, 2 June 1988

Fanny Hair
Born Texas, *c.*1882 (Marlow, Oklahoma, 1930 US census)

Pubecca Hare
Born Kent, *c.*1831 (Minster, Kent, 1841 England census)

Fanny Harris
Born np, nd (Fulham, London, 1911 England census)
*While coy about her place and date of birth, Fanny was happy to
reveal her profession in the 1911 census as 'prostitute'.*

Cunty Hoel
Born Warnham, Cheshire, *c.*1849
(Walton-on-the-Hill, Lancashire, 1871 England census)
Cunty Hoel was the wife of Dick Hoel.

Harry Hole
Born *c.*1843; passenger on *Neville*, London, England–Sydney,
Australia, arrived 11 September 1862

Cunt Holmatron
Married Etin Johnsen, Laporte, Indiana, USA, 28 August 1918

Cunt Honeycutt
Mother of Jack Honeycutt, born Jackson, North Carolina, USA,
1 April 1927

Labia Hood
Born Nottingham, *c.*1843
(Snelland, Nottinghamshire, 1861 England census)

Horny Cunt
(Female) Born *c.*1863 (Dakota Territory, 1886 US Indian census)

Mary Ann Cunt Hunt
Born Cheriton Fitzpaine, Devon, *c.*1829
(Thorverton, Devon, 1851 England census)
*Mary Ann and George F. Cunt Hunt were the parents of a
girl baptized three months earlier with the same rhyming name
as her mother.*

Mike Hunt
Born Chippenham, Wiltshire, 1842

York Hunt
Born Georgia, *c.*1845 (Pike, Georgia, 1870 US census)

Vaginas [*sic*] Jennings
Born Virginia, *c.*1876 (Manchester, Virginia, 1920 US census)

Vulva Johnson
Died Baldwin, Alabama, USA, 6 July 1947

Ka Ka Cunts Morgan
Born *c.*1850 (Oregon, 1891 US Indian census)

Merkin King
Born Nassington, Northamptonshire, *c.*1837
(Nassington, 1871 England census)
*A merkin is a pubic wig worn by prostitutes. The word first
appeared in print in English in 1617.*

Friedrich Cunt Koch
Married (spouse unknown), Brown, Wisconsin,
USA, 21 May 1877

Fannie Kunt
Born Clipstone, Nottinghamshire, *c.*1873
(Kirkby, Nottinghamshire, 1891 England census)

Harry Kunt
Born *c.*1908; passenger on *Leviathan*, Halifax, Nova Scotia,
Canada–New York, USA, arrived 27 July 1931

Adolph Kunty
Born Germany, *c.*1864 (Derby, 1891 England census)

See D. Kuntz
Born Pennsylvania, *c.*1906
(East Mahoning, Pennsylvania, 1920 US census)

Hervey Le Cunte
Of Norwich, Norfolk (Will, 1320–21)

Avagina Ledford
Born North Carolina, *c.*1832
(Cherokee, North Carolina, 1850 US census)

Harry Broad Cunt Lightowlers
Born Stainland, Yorkshire, *c.*1907
(Huddersfield, Yorkshire, 1911 England census)

Cunt Lindberg
Born Massachusetts, 1894
(Worcester City, Massachusetts, 1900 US census)

Fanny Lips
Married John Christophers, Falmouth, Cornwall, 13 April 1823

C. Litoris
Baptized Liebfrauen Katholisch, Koblenz, Prussia,
29 September 1602

Jennings McCunt
Married Julia Little, Calhoun, West Virginia, USA, 18 March 1883

Pussy Memory
Born North Carolina, 1860
(Cumberland, North Carolina, 1860 US census)

Fanny Merkin
Born Thingoe, Suffolk, 1845

Max Merkin
Born Poland, *c.*1877 (Elizabeth, New Jersey, 1930 US census)
Max Merkin was the husband of Minnie Merkin.

Minnie Merkin
Born Poland, *c.*1879
(Elizabeth, New Jersey, 1930 US census)

Fanny Minge
Born Italy, *c.*1873
(Somerset, New Jersey, 1920 US census)

Guldbrand Minge
Married Maria Ramstad, Tune, Ostfold,
Norway, 20 November 1782

Harry Minge
Born *c.*1895 (Roselle, New Jersey, 1930 US census)
He also had a son, Harry Minge Jr, born c.*1923.*

Harrye Minge
Married Catherine Jefferye, Horsemonden, Kent, 23 October 1559

Meta Alwine Minge
Born Harrogate, South Australia, 31 December 1897;
died 28 October 1994

Patience Minge
Married Richard Polle, St Mary Bredin, Canterbury,
Kent, 28 August 1662

Minge Bacon
(Male) Born *c.*1910 (Nevada, 1912 US Indian census)

Minge Semon
(Male) Born *c.*1881 (Isleta, New Mexico, 1886 US Indian census)

Archimedes Muff
Married Dewsbury, Yorkshire, 1848

Fanny Muff
Born Leeds, Yorkshire, *c.*1846
(Wortley, Yorkshire, 1871 England census)

Harry Muff

Born England, *c.*1892 (Minneapolis, Minnesota, 1930 US census)
Harry Muff was the husband of Berdie Muff.

Cunts Munts

(Female) Born Germany, *c.*1815
(Richfield, Washington, Wisconsin, 1850 US census)

Vagina O'Hara

Born *c.*1891 (San Francisco, California, 1920 US census)

Opens Her Cunt (aka Makes It Fart)

(Female) Born *c.*1863 (Dakota Territory, 1886 US Indian census)

Fanny Organ

Born Frome, Somerset, 1838

Cunny Overend

(Female) Born Birkenhead, Cheshire, *c.*1870
(Birkenhead, 1871 England census)
*Cunny is a diminutive of Cunt; it is found to this day as a rare
surname, principally in the Manchester area.*

Fanny Passage

Born Sheerness, Kent, *c.*1865
(Gillingham, Kent, 1891 England census)

Born Alabama, *c.*1891 (Sawyerville, Alabama, 1920 US census)

Mary Plenty Holes

Married John Mesteth, Shannon, South Dakota, USA, 17 July 1915
*The Plenty Holes were a distinguished Lakota tribe family (Crazy
Horse and Sitting Bull were also members of the Lakota tribe).
Eddie Plenty Holes is the subject of a much-reproduced
photographic portrait dating from 1899.*

Vagina Price

Born Georgia, 1860
(Ring Jaw, Georgia, 1900 US census)

Ophelia Pubes

Born Louisiana, *c.*1825
(Assumption, Louisiana, 1870 US census)

Twing G. Pubis

Married Clara G. Kary, Minnehaha, South Dakota,
USA, 25 August 1924

Willy Punani

Born Hikueru, Tuamotu, French Polynesia, 1847

Seymour Pusey

Born India, *c.*1874 (Bedford,
1891 England census)

Fanny Pussey

Born Yorkshire, *c.*1817
(Holderness, Yorkshire, 1841
England census)

Harry Pussey

Born Croydon, Surrey, *c.*1863
(Croydon, 1901 England
census)

Joline Violet Pussy

Born 27 January 1889;
baptized 25 December 1889,
Rangoon, Burma

Fanny Quim
Born Georgia, *c*.1855 (Schley, Georgia, 1870 US census)

Pube Russell
(Female) Born Nova Scotia, Canada, 1904
(Lunenberg, Nova Scotia, 1911 Canada census)

Pudendiana Ryan
(Female) Born Viracapatam, India (Bury, Lancashire, 1891
England census)

Fanny Shaver
Married Stockton-on-Tees, Durham, 1842

Peter Twatt Shearer
Married Hampstead, London, 1900

Slippery Cunt
(Female) Born *c*.1858 (Dakota Territory, 1886 US Indian census)

Vagina Smith
Born Maryland, *c*.1824 (New York, 1870 US census)

Lucy Snatch
Married Robert Colley, St Dunstan, Stepney,
London, 11 June 1644

G. Spot
Married Frank M. Dendeen, Clare, Michigan, USA, 6 June 1897

Jennie Talia
Born *c*.1906 (Brooklyn, New York, 1930 US census)

Jennie Talls
Born Nebraska, 1899 (Douglas, Nebraska, 1900 US census)

Euphemia Twat
Baptized Walls, Shetland, 1800

*There were forty-eight Twats in Orkney and Shetland at the time of
the 1841 Scotland census. In this same year, in his poem 'Pippa Passes',
Robert Browning included the line 'Cowls and twats', later naively
explaining to the editor of the* Oxford English Dictionary *that he
thought a 'twat' was a kind of hood worn by nuns.*

Magnus Twatt
Born Walls, Shetland, *c.*1835 (Walls, 1881 Scotland census)

Phila Twatt
(Female) Born Orkney, *c.*1828 (Orkney, 1841 Scotland census)

Anna Vagina
Born Rivarolo, Italy, *c.*1875; passenger on *Chicago*, Le Havre,
France–New York, USA, arrived 29 March 1910

Arthur Vagina
Born Québec, June 1911 (Québec, 1911 Canada census)

Lucy Vagina
Born Italy, 1887 (Almeda, California, 1900 US census)

Labia Vanhorn
Born Pennsylvania, *c.*1821
(Philadelphia, Pennsylvania, 1860 US census)

Fannie Vulva
Born Iowa, 1885 (Putnam Township, Iowa, 1900 US census)

Fanny Watmuff
Born Bradford, Yorkshire, *c.*1863
(Cottingley, Yorkshire, 1871 England census)

Avagina White
Born San Mateo, California, USA, 8 July 1908

Cunty Young
Born New Hampshire, *c.*1815
(Bradleysvale, Vermont, 1850 US census)

KEEPING ABREAST

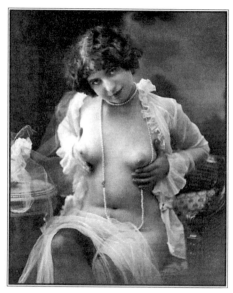

Synonyms for breasts – hooters, boobs, bristols, tits and so on – are surprisingly common as both first names and surnames, though none combine the two – the perfect pair therefore remains an elusive quarry.

Fanny Baps
Born North Carolina, *c.*1832
(Robeson, North Carolina, 1850 US census)

Elizabeth Boobies
Married Lewis Pearse, West Anstey, Devon, 25 January 1682

Mary Boobs
Born Peshwar, West Bengal, India, 11 April 1872
She was the daughter of John and Mary Boobs.

Meloina Boobs
Married John Stump, Meigs, Ohio, USA, 5 December 1865

Annys Bosom
Baptized St Mary the Virgin, Dover, Kent, 10 December 1589

Alice Maud Bristols
Born Mortlake, Surrey, c.1883
(Tenterden, Kent, 1911 England census)

Bertha Bristols
Born Charleston, South Carolina, USA, 20 November 1894

Jemima Busty
Married Denis Boston, Hampton-in-Arden, Warwickshire,
25 November 1819

Mary Buxom
Baptized Bombay, India, 5 June 1834

Ellen Bristol Dancer
Born Stoke-on-Trent, Staffordshire, 1860

Jugs Ferner
Born Scotland, c.1896 (East Ham, Essex, 1901 England census)

Maria de las Mercedes Globes
Born Santiago, Chile, 26 October 1887

Anna Hooters
Born Florida, c.1885
(Marion, Florida, USA, 1935 Florida state census)

Joanna Jugs
Born Massachusetts, c.1844 (Lewiston, Maine, 1880 US census)

Rose Knipples
Married James Mieras, Plymouth, Iowa, USA, 15 October 1898

Jan Knockers
Married Catharina Brienen, Hervormde Kerk, Nijmegen,
Netherlands, 22 November 1747

Mammary Label
Born New Brunswick, 1898 (New Brunswick, 1911 Canada census)

Large Breast
(Female) Born c.1839 (Idaho, 1897 US Indian census)

Long Face New Breast
Born c.1852 (Montana, 1914 US Indian census)

Jugs Lykken
(Female) Born Russia, c.1864; passenger on *Arabic*, Liverpool,
England–New York, USA, arrived 30 April 1888

Melons Meakin
Married Basford, Nottinghamshire, 1897

Mary Melons
Married Thomas Jones, Talgarth, Brecon, Wales, 19 February 1798

Mary Booby Morris
Born c.1827; died Weymouth, Dorset, 1896

Felton Nipples
Born Louisiana, *c.*1923 (New Orleans, Louisiana, 1930 US census)

Nancy Norks
Born Scotland, *c.*1836; passenger on *Glasgow*, Liverpool,
England–New York, USA, arrived 5 September 1861

Anice Pair
Born Georgia, *c.*1889 (Scottsboro, Alabama, 1920 US census)

See-Tu-Lee-Lah-Wee-Tits
(Male) Recipient of Civil War pension, 1894

Gloria Stitz
Divorced from Howard Stitz, Bexar, Texas, USA,
17 December 1990

Norma Stitz
Born *c.*1824 (Benton, Indiana, 1930 US census)

Janita Tit
Born Netherlands, c.1872; passenger on *Westernland*, Antwerp, Belgium–New York, USA, arrived 22 February 1932

Hugh Tits
Born np, nd (Shamokin, Northumberland, Pennsylvania, 1830 US census)

Hugo Tits
Baptized Araraquara, São Paulo, Brazil, 15 December 1903; died 5 February 1976

Titus Tits
Married Jane Bodet, New York, America, 1726

Tits Down
(Female) Born c.1848 (Montana, 1897 US Indian census)

Dorothea Titties
Born Beaufort West, Cape of Good Hope, South Africa, c.1816

Pleasant Titty
Daughter of Thomas and Pleasant Titty, baptized St John, Margate, Kent, 3 April 1768
Her birth meant there was a pair of Pleasant Tittys in the family.

Rosanna Udders
Born np, nd; convicted in York; transported on *Friendship*, arrived New South Wales, Australia, January 1818 (*New South Wales and Tasmania, Australia, Settler and Convict Lists 1787–1834*)

Areola Vice
Born South Carolina, c.1894
(St Johns, South Carolina, 1910 US census)

Titties Wadsworth
Born New York, c.1876 (Brooklyn, New York, 1910 US census)

Allice [*sic*] Whoppers
Baptized St Nicholas, Gloucester, 22 December 1578

A BIT OF HOW'S YOUR FATHER

A step on from finding yourself named after an intimate body part would be to have a name that describes – often quite graphically – sounds like or suggests sexual activity of one sort or another. You or I would change it, but most of these people somehow muddled through…

Fanny Action
Baptized Claverley, Shropshire, 22 April 1747

Juan Afuck
Born *c*.1847; passenger on *Santiago*, Havana, Cuba–New York, USA, arrived 11 July 1883

Fuck Ah
Born China, 6 June 1854
(New Westminster, British Columbia, 1901 Canada census)
See also: Ah Fuck.

Ann Ally
Born Massachusetts, *c.*1820 (Lynn, Massachusetts, 1870 US census)

Marie Dolores Anal
Married Francisco Lopes, Santa Maria De Los Reyes,
Huatlatlauca, Puebla, Mexico, 9 January 1878

Henriette Anus
Married Jean Batiste Boulfrois, Saint-Aignan, France,
11 February 1738

Dick Anybody
Married Margreett [*sic*] Gaskine, Rowley Regis,
Staffordshire, 1 January 1668

Ofelia Arce
Baptized La Merced, Chachapoyas, Peru, 15 March 1890

Dick Ass
Born Kolberg, Prussia, 23 November 1881;
died 24 November 1941

Healen [sic] Asslick
Married John Bewley, St Nicholas, Liverpool, 12 April 1835

Felia Ball
Born North Carolina, *c.*1880
(Leicester, South Carolina, 1910 US census)

Dick Balling
Born Alabama, 1909 (Greenville, Alabama, 1910 US census)

Isaac Balls
Born Lexden, Essex, 1839

Ophelia Balls
Born Georgia, *c.*1885 (Chatham, Georgia, 1910 US census)

Ellen Ballswell
Born Ohio, *c.*1845 (Richmond, Missouri, 1880 US census)

Ava Bang
Born Yugoslavia, *c.*1903; passenger on *Melita*, Antwerp,
Belgium–Montreal, Canada, arrived 15 May 1926

Bertha Bangs
Born Nebraska, *c.*1885 (Lincoln, Nebraska, 1910 US census)

Dick Bangs
Born Michigan, *c.*1911 (Paw Paw, Michigan, 1920 US census)

Rut Bare
Born Rännelanda, Sweden, 4 October 1909

Spunk Beard
(Male) Born *c.*1926 (Lincoln, Mississippi, 1930 US census)

Etta Beaver
Born Washington, *c.*1892
(West Montesano, Washington, 1910 US census)

Isaac Beaver
Born Pickering, Yorkshire, 1898

Love Beaver
(Male) Born North Carolina, *c.*1903
(China Grove, North Carolina, 1920 US census)

Ophelia Beaver
Born North Carolina, USA, 3 September 1928

Susannah Bedswell
Married James Wyand, Bosmere, Suffolk, 1849

Betsy Cockin Beevers
Died Huddersfield, Yorkshire, 1852

Fanny Bendova
Born Italy, *c.*1876 (New Haven, Connecticut, 1910 US census)

Bites As He Sucks
Born *c.*1839 (Sioux, South Dakota, 1896 US Indian census)

Eatme Blechart
Born *c.*1861 (Montpelier, Idaho, 1930 US census)

Dick Blower
Baptized Roxwell, Essex, 19 September 1559

Abigail Bondage
Married David Pratt Jr, Bridgewater, Massachusetts,
America, 12 April 1753

Dick Bondage
Born Woolwich, London, *c.*1882 (Woolwich, 1901 England census)

Daily Boner
(Female) Born Hernhill, Kent, *c.*1898
(Hernhill, 1901 England census)

Dick Boner
Born Missouri, *c.*1909 (Phoenix, Arizona, 1930 US census)

Hugh Boner
Married Mary Silk, Baltimore, Maryland, USA, 12 August 1796

Wincenty Bonk
Born Poland, *c.*1893 (Detroit, Michigan, 1930 US census)

Hepzibah Bonker
Born *c.*1826 (Barton Seagrave, Northamptonshire, 1841 census)

Dick Bonking
Married Elizabeth Feldhousen, Baltimore, Maryland,
USA, 24 July 1821

Lulu Bonks
Born Illinois, 1877 (New York, 1900 US census)

Lou Bricant
(Female) Born Pitton, Wiltshire, *c*.1807
(Pitton, 1871 England census)
Lou Bricant also had a daughter of the same name.

Ophelia Bristol
Born Michigan, 1857 (Otisco, Ionia, Michigan, 1900 US census)

Edith Buggery
Resident of Bourke, Victoria, 1903 (1901–36 Australian electoral rolls)

Fanny Buggery
Born Wendover, Buckinghamshire, *c*.1891
(Harrow on the Hill, Middlesex, 1911 England census)

Harvey Bukake
Born *c*.1887; passenger on *Hororata*, Melbourne–Sydney,
Australia, arrived 20 March 1916
Bukake or bukkake originated in Japan and is popular in
pornography but is rarely practised in the better households.

Randy Bumpass
Died Waller, Texas, USA, 25 October 1977

Ophelia Butt
Born Tennessee, *c.*1879 (Maury, Tennessee, 1880 US census)
Ophelia Butt was the sister of Willy Butt.

Sex Butter
(Male) Born Georgia, 1883
(Savannah City, Georgia, 1900 US census)

Rossool Bux Fucker Bux
Born *c.*1889; passenger on *Obra*, Calcutta, India–Sydney,
Australia, arrived 14 November 1914

Clifton Carnal
Born *c.*1921 (Slaughtersville, Webster, Kentucky, 1930 US census)

Sexy Chambers
(Female) Born Texas, *c.*1905 (Roxton, Lamar, Texas, 1910 US census)
Sexy was the sister of Fannie, Dewey, Roxie and Johnie [sic]
Chambers.

Buster Cherry
Born Mississippi, *c.*1880 (Lee, Mississippi, 1920 US census)

John Benjamin Fister Christian
Born Eastry, Kent, 1859

William Deviant Christie
Born Hackney, London, 1845

Stiffie Clews
(Female) Born Flint, *c.*1886 (Flint, 1901 Wales census)

Nora Climax
Born *c.*1894 (Harris, Texas, 1930 US census)

Ada Cock
Born Penzance, Cornwall, 1866

Alice Ada Cock
Born Wapping, London, *c.*1846
(Covent Garden, London, 1871 England census)

Henrietta Cock
Baptized Feock, Cornwall, 11 April 1830

Juliette Cock
Born Belgium, *c.*1877; passenger on *Finland*, Liverpool,
England–New York, USA, arrived 13 September 1914

Love Cock
(Female) Daughter of Gabriel Cock, baptized St Columb Major,
Cornwall, 3 June 1659

Nora Cock
Born *c.*1899 (St Pancras, London, 1911 England census)

Rhoda Cock
Married Thomas Lovack, South Lopham, Norfolk, 9 February 1815

Rosetta Cock
Born Vermont, *c.*1815 (Monkton, Vermont, 1850 US census)

Sukey Cock
Married Samuel Brown, St Mary, Truro, Cornwall, 27 March 1826

Zach Cock
Born Kingsessing, Philadelphia, 1674

Ellen Fanny Cockaday
Born Norwich, Norfolk, 23 June 1880

Percy Cockfit
Born Chelmsford, Essex, 1867

Mary Cockfull
Died Huddersfield, Yorkshire, 1852

Ulaya Cockin
Baptized St Agnes, Cornwall, 9 December 1673

Dick Cockout
Baptized Manchester Cathedral, Manchester, Lancashire, 17 May 1796

Minnie Cockswell
Born Kings Norton, Leicestershire, *c.*1828
(Bournemouth, Hampshire, 1891 England census)

Fanny Cockup
Born Dartford, Kent, 1840

Emma Lovina Cockwell
Born Ontario, Canada, 19 August 1869

Minnie Coitus
Born Holland, *c.*1893 (Saskatchewan, Canada, 1916 Manitoba,
Saskatchewan and Alberta census)

Ofelia Comes
Born Spain, *c.*1894; passenger on *Antonio Lopez*, Havana,
Cuba–New York, USA, arrived 6 March 1924

Comes Inside
(Male) Born *c.*1875 (Dakota Territory, 1886 US Indian census)

Comes Twice
(Male) Born *c.*1894 (Montna, 1899 US Indian census)

Fanny Comewell
Born Kings Norton, Leicestershire, *c.*1828 (Bournemouth,
Hampshire, 1901 England census)

Curry Condom
Born Nova Scotia, Canada, *c.*1825

Jesus Condom
Born 28 September 1959; died Dade, Florida, USA, 23 June 1993

Willy Condom
Born Connecticut, *c.*1866
(New Haven, Connecticut, 1880 US census)

Semen Cox
Born New Jersey, *c.*1875 (Lower, New Jersey, 1920 US census)

Jean Creamer
Born 29 June 1929; died Plymouth, Devon, March 1989

John Cum
Born Hitchin, Hertfordshire, *c.*1850
(Essendon, Hertfordshire, 1871 England census)

Carlota Cumalot
Born 26 October 1868; baptized Torroella De Montgrí,
Girona, Spain, 29 October 1868

Juan Cumalot
Born *c.*1836; passenger on *Charles W. Lord*, Havana,
Cuba–New Orleans, Louisiana, USA, arrived 18 October 1875

Mari Anus Cuming
(Male) Born Scotland, 1845
(Brooklyn, New York, 1900 US census)
*His first name was Marianus but it was often split in this way
by him and other members of the Cuming family, several
of whom stoically bore it.*

E. I. M. Cumming
Born Scotland, *c.*1865
(Camberwell, London, 1891 England census)

Ima Cumming
Born Michigan, *c.*1866 (Johnstown, Michigan, 1880 US census)

Isie Cumming
Born Tomintoul, Banffshire, *c.*1844
(Tomintoul, 1891 Scotland census)

Ophelia Cumming
Born Georgia, *c.*1878 (Columbia, Georgia, 1880 US census)

Willy P. Cumpecker
Born Amsterdam Township, Botetourt, Virginia,
USA, 30 July 1870

John Cumshoe
Born Burnley, Lancashire, 1843

Bethiah Cunlick
Born Beaminster, Somerset, 1844

Rhoda Cunt
Born Tennessee, *c.*1863 (Tennessee, 1870 US census)

John Cuntsman
Born Bavaria, *c.*1830 (Carlinville, Illinois, 1880 US census)
Only two Cuntsman families are recorded in the USA: farmer
John Cuntsman and his wife Margret [sic] *lived with their nine*
children in Carlinville while Adin and Dena Cuntsman and
their two children were recorded in Jersey City, New Jersey.
Since none appear in subsequent censuses, we may assume they
all changed their surnames.

Molester Musky Davis
Born Johnson, North Carolina, USA, 7 November 1884;
died Wilson, North Carolina, USA, 17 November 1943

Daw Fucker
(Male) Born *c.*1859
(Cheyenne, Oklahoma, 1905 US Indian census)

Ernest Deflower
Born Charleroi, Belgium, *c.*1885; passenger on *Vaderland*, Antwerp,
Belgium–New York, USA, arrived 8 May 1907

Charles Deviant
Born England, *c.*1873; passenger on *Paris*, Southampton,
England–New York, USA, arrived 16 September 1895

Anita Dick
Born Mississippi, *c.*1889 (Jackson, Mississippi, 1910 US census)

Henrietta Dick
Born Birkenhead, Cheshire, 1900

Isaac Dick
Born Ohio, *c.*1854 (Cass, Ohio, 1880 US census)

Ivana Dick
Born c.1909 (Winterset, Iowa, 1930 US census)

Ophelia Dick
Born Alabama, 1857 (Mobile, Alabama, 1900 US census)

Rosetta Dick
Born Illinois, c.1856 (Hamilton, Iowa, 1870 US census)

Suckey Dick
(Female) Born South Carolina, c.1840
(Swimming Pens, Sumter, South Carolina, 1870 US census)

Henretta [sic] Dickass
Born Pennsylvania, c.1855
(O'Hara, Allegheny, Pennsylvania, 1880 US census)

John Large Dickin
Married Wem, Shropshire, 1870

Mary Dicklick
Born Alabama, c.1907
(Cunningham Precinct, Alabama, 1920 US census)

Isaac Dicks
Born New York, c.1793
(Poughkeepsie, New York, 1870 US census)

Harriet Dickswell
Born c.1856 (New Bedford, Massachusetts, 1920 US census)

Willy Dickus
Born Ohio, c.1828 (Perry, Ohio, 1850 US census)

Fanny Dickwell
Born Butterwick, Lincolnshire, c.1859
(Leake, Lincolnshire, 1861 England census)
*Fanny was the daughter of Willy Dickwell Sr and sister
of Willy Dickwell Jr.*

Amanda Dildo
Married James C. McElfresh, Jackson, Illinois,
USA, 16 February 1860

Magdalina Lanonia Dildo
Baptized San Sebastian Cathedral, Bacolod City,
Philippines, 19 May 1781

Bridget Dogging
Born Ireland, *c.*1869 (Barony, Lanarkshire, 1891 Scotland census)
The etymology of the British slang term 'dogging' – engaging in
sex in public places – has not yet been definitively established.
One school of thought claims it derives from the common response
of men caught in search of such activities, as participant or
voyeur, 'I was just walking the dog...'

Fellate Dube
Born California, *c.*1874 (San Francisco, 1910 US census)

Fanny Eater
Born *c.*1816 (Hampstead, London, 1841 England census)
She is possibly the same Fanny Eater who shows up in the 1860
US census, in Middleborough, Plymouth, Massachusetts,
as born in England in c.1815. Could she have been driven to
emigrate by jokes about her name?

Peter Eater
Born Pennsylvania, *c.*1868
(Lower Allen, Pennsylvania, 1920 US census)

Eatme Edwards
(Female) Born *c.*1827 (Amlwch, Anglesey, 1841 Wales census)

Willy Ejack
Born Pennsylvania, *c.*1886
(Pittsburgh, Pennsylvania, 1910 US census)

Rufina Facial
Born Hinundayan, Leyte, Philippines, 1870

Fanny Man Eater
(Female) Born *c.*1875 (Nebraska, 1897 US Indian census)

Antonino Felati
Born Italy, *c.*1872; passenger on *Neckar*, Naples, Italy–New York,
USA, arrived 15 March 1907

Nicholas Felcher
Born Denmark, c.1826 (Harrison, Mississippi, 1860 US census)
*The practice of felching is too disgusting to explain here – buy
yourself a good slang dictionary (see page 13).*

Ease Fellate
(Male) Born Ireland, c.1875 (Stevens, Montana, 1910 US census)

Elizabeth Fellater
Born Adamston, Ontario, Canada; died Renfrew, Ontario,
Canada, 8 November 1921

William Fellator
Born Ireland, c.1825
(Wyandotte, Butte, California, 1880 US census)

Henry Feltbush
Born Posey, Indiana, USA, 11 September 1907

Fanny Filler
Born New York, c.1847 (New York, 1870 US census)

Will Fillerup
Born Illinois, c.1878 (Leon, Iowa, 1895 Iowa state census)

Dick Firm
Born c.1861 (Penge, London, 1891 England census)

Dick Fits
Born Sandown Township, Rockingham, New Hampshire,
America, 8 August 1758

Victor Fitsin
Application for US naturalization, New York, USA, 3 July 1882

John Carnal Fox
Married Stoke-on-Trent, Staffordshire, 1851

Bumming Frederick
Born Great Hanningfield, Suffolk, c.1830
(Colchester, Essex, 1901 England census)

Quick French
Died Eastbourne, Sussex, 1881

Anna Quick Fuchs
Born Bremen, Germany, 14 February 1883
(2 January 1906–31 March 1925 US passport applications)

Ah Fuck
Born China, *c.*1829 (Drytown, California, 1860 US census)
See also: Fuck Ah.

Earnest Willie Fuck
Born Davenport, Scott, Iowa, USA, 23 February 1895

Everhard Fuck
Born Friesheim, Germany, 23 April 1856

Fanny Fuck
Married Vite Epstein, Cooper, Missouri, USA, 20 November 1851

Lino Fuck
Baptized São Pedro De Alcântara, Santa Catarina,
Brazil, 24 February 1897

Maria Fuck
Born Stolberg, Germany, 19 November 1890;
died Epichnellen, Germany, 24 May 1945

Pleasant Fuck
(Male) Born Missouri, *c.*1859
(Blackwater, Pettis, Missouri, 1870 US census)

Wong Fuck
(Male) Born China, 1827
(San Francisco, California, 1880 US census)

Louis Fuckall
Born *c.*1881; passenger on *Ionian*, St John, Canada–Liverpool,
England, arrived January 1908

Adolf Fuckar
Born Moslavina, Croatia, *c.*1912; passenger on *Belvedere*, Trieste,
Italy–New York, USA, arrived 17 January 1921

Annie Fucked
Born Alabama, *c.*1904 (Chambers, Alabama, 1930 US census)

Fanny Fucker
Born *c*.1872; passenger on *Lusitania*, Liverpool, England–New York, USA, arrived 28 March 1908

Mercy Fucker
Born Kent, *c*.1835 (Mayland, Essex, 1861 England census)

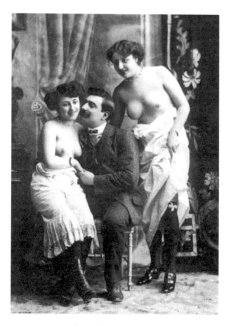

Randy Fucker
Father born Naples, Italy, *c*.1879; son, Randy Fucker Jr, born Boston, Massachusetts, USA, *c*.1914; passengers on *Dulio*, Naples, Italy–New York, USA, arrived 27 September 1925

Hugh Fuckhouse
Born Indiana, *c*.1854 (Indianapolis, Indiana, 1900 US census)

Hattie Fucki
Born Nevada, *c*.1880 (Roseville, California, 1920 US census)

Archibald Fucking

Born England, *c.*1904; passenger on *Albania*, London,
England–New York, USA, arrived 13 November 1924

Christ Fuckinger

Born Germany, *c.*1820; passenger on *Hansa*, Bremen,
Germany–New York, USA, arrived 2 April 1874

Harry Fuckingham

Born Ashover, Chesterfield, *c.*1859
(Chesterfield, 1911 England census)

Michael Fuckit

Born *c.*1900 (New York, 1920 US census)

Werner Fuckman

Born New York City, USA, 24 March 1897

Jean Pierre Fuckmes

Born Germany, *c.*1882; passenger on *Vaderland*, Antwerp,
Belgium–New York, USA, arrived 3 July 1907

Filomena Fucko

Born Italy, *c.*1855
(Youngstown, Ohio, 1920 US census)

Annie Fucks

Born *c.*1872; passenger on *Lake Ontario*, Liverpool,
England–Halifax, Nova Scotia, Canada, arrived 7 December 1900

Ernest Fucks

Born Germany, *c.*1882 (Maidstone, Kent, 1911 England census)
*Ernest's profession, as listed in the 1911 census, was
'intensive gardening'; he was the husband of Violet Fucks,
born Victoria, Australia, c.1879.*

Max Fucks

Born Russia, *c.*1888; passenger on *Kaiser Wilhelm II*, Bremen,
Germany–New York, USA, arrived 10 May 1907

Ceamon Fuckwell

Born *c.*1885 (Merrimac, Massachusetts, 1930 US census)

Jemima Fukin
Born Penzance, Cornwall, *c.*1801 (Derby, 1851 England census)

Minnie Fukins
Born London, *c.*1847 (Aldington, Kent, 1861 England census)

William Fukmadge
Married Joan Crann, Netherbury, Dorset, 22 September 1818

Mary Fuxall
Born Virginia, *c.*1849 (South Wheeling, Virginia, 1860 US census)

Jane Fuxlonger
Born London, *c.*1803 (Lambeth, London, 1871 England census)

Charlotte Gobbles
Born Chatham, Kent, *c.*1873 (Chatham, 1891 England census)

Dick Gobling
Born Croydon, Surrey, *c.*1810
(Lewisham, London, 1881 England census)

Sarah Godown
Baptized St Dunstan, Stepney, London, 1 April 1710

Fanny Goodhead
Born Burton upon Trent, Staffordshire, 1848

A. Goodlay
Born Ireland, *c.*1832 (St Louis, Missouri, 1860 US census)

Lucinda Goodtime
Born Perry, Ohio, USA, 1884

Isuck Gordon
(Male) Born Alabama, *c.*1867 (Alabama, 1870 US census)

Oral Gordon
Born Oklahoma, *c.*1912
(Warren Valley, Oklahoma, 1930 US census)

Willie Gothard
Born Alabama, *c.*1875 (Randolph, Alabama, 1910 US census)

Condoms Grace
(Male) Born Mississippi, *c.*1868
(Hamburg, Mississippi, 1880 US census)

Willy Growcocks
Baptized Cheswardine, Shropshire, 24 September 1691

Growls As She Comes
Born *c.*1886 (South Dakota, 1892 US Indian census)

Debbie Gulps
Born New York, USA, *c.*1861; married Benjamine [*sic*] Palmer,
Sparta, Michigan, USA, 18 February 1877

Fanny Hammer
Born Wisconsin, *c.*1863
(Milwaukee, Wisconsin, 1900 US census)

Straiton Hard
(Male) Born New York, USA, 28 November 1884

Dick Hardcock
Born *c.*1791 (Cheltenham, Gloucestershire, 1841 England census)

Willy Harddick
Born 1867 (Halfmoon, Saratoga, New York, 1900 US census)

Ophelia Harden
Born Louisiana, *c.*1890 (Hardy, Louisiana, 1920 US census)

Bent Hardon
Born Vermont, *c.*1848 (Vermont, 1860 US census)

Fanny Hardon
Born Lancaster, Lancashire, *c.*1904
(Lancaster, 1911 England census)
Fanny was the daughter of Minnie Hardon (born c.1868)
and sister of another Minnie Hardon (born c.1902) and
Norah Hardon (born c.1909).

Ivor Hardon
Born Llansamlet, Glamorgan, *c.*1878
(Swansea, Glamorgan, 1891 Wales census)

Penis Hardon
(Male) Born Ireland, *c.*1811
(Fulham, London, 1851 England census)

Isaac Hiscock
Born Dorset, *c.*1831
(Tarrant Gunville, Dorset, 1841 England census)

Love Hiscock
Baptized Mere, Wiltshire, 18 April 1825

Ophelia Fanny Hole
Married Weymouth, Dorset, 1860

Phyllis Private Holes
Born Eastbourne, Sussex, 1893

Anita Hooker
Born Louisiana, *c.*1907 (New Orleans, Louisiana, 1910 US census)

Ima Hooker
Born Texas, *c.*1896 (Rusk, Texas, 1910 US census)

Tiny Hooker
Born Mississippi, 1887 (Pontotoc, Mississippi, 1900 US census)

Iva Horn
Born *c.*1882; passenger on *Berengaria*, New York,
USA–Southampton, England, arrived 17 August 1927

Anna Humpalova
Born Březí, Bohemia, *c.*1883; passenger on *Kaiser Wilhelm II*,
Bremen, Germany–New York, USA, arrived 13 October 1903

Rose Humps
Born Essex, *c.*1889
(Southend-on-Sea, Essex, 1911 England census)

Harlot Hunt
(Male) Born Nova Scotia, 27 June 1894
(Colchester, Nova Scotia, 1901 Canada census)

Beaver Hunter
Born Georgia, *c.*1894 (Grove Creek, Georgia, 1910 US census)

Fanny Hunter
Born Rye, Kent, 1838

Fanny Hustler
Baptized Pudsey, Yorkshire, 18 December 1785

Will Icome
Born Whitechapel, London, 1856

Dick Inass
Born Washington, *c.*1877 (Lewis, Washington, 1880 US census)

Trifgen Jism
Born Macedonia, *c.*1882
(Franklin, Columbus, Ohio, 1910 US census)

Blo Job
Born Slovakia, *c.*1897; passenger on *La Bretagne*, Le Havre,
France–New York, USA, arrived 21 December 1903

Fuk Jordan
(Male) Born *c.*1879 (Oregon, 1886 US Indian census)

Caty Cumsin Josey
Born Rowan County, North Carolina, USA, *c.*1781

Fu King
Born *c.*1917; passenger on *San Simeon*, Liverpool,
England–New York, USA, arrived 4 July 1942

Hyman Kitoff
Born 10 August 1893; died Dade, Florida, USA,
29 September 1976

Suck Kock
Born China, *c.*1892; passenger on *Nippon Maru*, Hong Kong–San
Francisco, California, USA, arrived 22 September 1913

Chase Kuntz
Born Pennsylvania, *c.*1866
(Lancaster, Pennsylvania, 1920 US census)

Semen Kuntze
(Male) Born Waterbury, Connecticut, USA, *c.*1906; passenger
on *New York*, Southampton, England–New York, USA, arrived
28 February 1913

Ophelia Kunz
Born Georgia, *c.*1878 (Houston, Georgia, 1910 US census)

Fanny Lapping
Born 14 September 1888; died Pomona, California, USA,
30 October 1974

Analey Larking
Died Sevenoaks, Kent, 1843

Fanny E. C. Lay
Born South Carolina, *c.*1877
(Dogwood Neck, South Carolina, 1880 US census)

Peculiar Lay
(Female) Born *c.*1820
(Kit Carson, Greenwood, Colorado, 1870 US census)

Earnest Lecher
Born *c.*1910 (Easton, Pennsylvania, 1930 US census)

Augusta Lefuck
Born Estonia, *c.*1890; passenger on *Augusta W. Snow*, Halifax,
Nova Scotia, Canada–New York, USA, arrived 25 June 1925

Lydia Legover
Born Illinois, *c.*1871 (Esmen, Livingston, Illinois, 1910 US census)

Mo Lester
Born Georgia, *c.*1828 (Dooly, Georgia, 1870 US census)

Hanah Lickass
Married Edward Rowling, York, 20 April 1777

Mary Lickcock
Married Mike Warso, Mercer, Pennsylvania, USA, 28 June 1892

Dick Licker
Born Oldham, Lancashire, *c.*1845 (Oldham, 1861 England census)

Fanny Licker
Born Kentucky, 1885 (Louisville, Kentucky, 1900 US census)

Dick Licks
Married Jenny Clen-Quit-Sun, Clallam, Washington,
USA, 18 May 1878

Licks Every Body
(Female) Born *c.*1864 (Idaho, 1891 US Indian census)

Lies In Bed With A Man
(Female) Born *c.*1857 (Montana, 1913 US Indian census)

Connie Linger
Born Wolverhampton, Staffordshire, *c.*1889
(Birmingham, Warwickshire, 1891 England census)

Connie Lingua
Born *c.*1926 (Brooklyn, New York, 1930 US census)

Free Love

Married Almette Almentha Miller, Cape Girardeau,
Missouri, USA, 25 May 1939

Oral Love

(Male) Born Texas, *c.*1893
(Rockwall, Texas, 1910 US census)

Dick Lover

Born South Carolina, *c.*1888
(Chickamauga, Georgia, 1930 US census)

Elizabeth Lovescock

Baptized St Giles Cripplegate, London,
21 February 1727

Mary Lovesit

Married Thomas Goldsmith, Trinity Church, New York, USA,
20 October 1784

Alberta Lovetoy
Born Windsor, Berkshire, *c.*1879
(Plumstead, London, 1891 England census)

Fanny Loving
Born Isle of Wight, Hampshire, 1841

Barney Lube
Born Kansas, *c.*1863 (Kit Carson, Colorado, 1930 US census)

Lucy Lube
Born Preston, Lancashire, *c.*1830
(Formby, Lancashire, 1881 England census)

Max Lubed
Married Edith Herd, St Marylebone, London, 1918

Lucy Comes Behind
Born *c.*1874 (South Dakota, 1895 US Indian census)

Herbert Lusty Lusty
Born Stroud, Gloucestershire, 1902

Stuffs McAnally
(Male) Born Georgia, 1895
(Abbeville Town, Georgia, 1900 US census)

Phil McCracken
Born Lewisham, Kent, *c.*1877 (Lewisham, 1911 England census)

Willy McCum
Born Bolton, Lancashire, 1840

Emma McDildo
Born West Virginia, *c.*1885
(Carroll, West Virginia, 1920 US census)

Mountable McGhee
(Male) Born Tennessee, *c.*1889
(Campbell, Tennessee, 1900 US census)

Archibald McRim
Born Chorley, Lancashire, 1865

Kenneth McShager
Born Scotland, *c.*1811
(Glasgow, Lanarkshire, 1841 Scotland census)

Frederick Randy Major
Born Aspull, Cheshire, *c.*1906
(Nantwich, Cheshire, 1911 England census)

Roger Mee
Died Bolton, Lancashire, 1856

Fuk Mi
Died British Columbia, Canada, 16 March 1894

Erotica Morales
Born Puerto Rico *c.*1898 (Rio Prieto, Puerto Rico, 1930 US census)

Comes More
Born Middlesex, *c.*1821
(Covent Garden, London, 1841 England census)

Love Morehead
(Male) Born North Carolina, *c.*1910
(Guilford, North Carolina, 1930 US census)

Randi Munch
Baptized Norderhov, Norway, 15 January 1736

Dick Muncher
Born Welshampton, Shropshire, *c.*1838
(Horseman's Green, Flintshire, 1891 Wales census)

Fanny Muncher
Born *c.*1912 (Watters, Georgia, 1930 US census)

Georgina Munchmore
Born *c.*1867; died Watford, Hertfordshire, 1903

Dick Myass
Baptized Hornsea, Yorkshire, 26 January 1804

Harold Candle Mycock
Died Lewisham, London, 1879

Isaac Mycock
Son of Reuben Mycock, baptized Buxton, Derbyshire, 1876

Martha Rogers Mycock
Married Rotherham, Yorkshire, 1887

Roger Mycock
Born Leeds, Yorkshire, 1913

Roger Myring
Convicted Stafford, 26 February 1801; transported on *Glatton* to New South Wales, Australia, 1802–03

Rosetta Nipple
Born Ohio, *c.*1838 (Decatur, Green, Wisconsin, 1850 US census)

Etta Nipples
Born c.1897 (Escambia, Florida, 1935 Florida state census)

Edna Nooky
Born Alabama, c.1894 (Chambers, Alabama, 1930 US census)

Obscene
(Male) Born c.1872 (Arizona, 1885 US Indian census)
Obscene, a member of the Mohave tribe, was the son of Beaver.

Fuck On
Born China, c.1852 (Treasure City, Nevada, 1870 US census)

Charlotte Openbottom
Married Step Easley, Centenary Methodist Episcopal Church
South, Palestine, Anderson, Texas, USA, 27 July 1881

Fanny Oral
Born Campbell, Kentucky, USA, 8 January 1861

Willy Orally
Born Massachusetts, c.1869
(Medway, Massachusetts, 1870 US census)

Gustavo Orgasmucci
Born Italy, c.1892; passenger on *Verona*, Naples, Italy–New York,
USA, arrived 9 April 1914

Nicholas Orgy
Baptized St Martin-in-the-Fields, London, 26 December 1626

Elizabeth Spunk Oxley
Born Dewsbury, Yorkshire, 1871

Humping M. C. Palmer
(Male) Born Newbury, Berkshire, c.1872
(Newbury, 1881 England census)

Pays For Her Trouble
Born c.1868 (Montana, 1897 US Indian census)
Pays For Her Trouble was the wife of Curley Bear.

Rhoda Penis
Born Tennessee, c.1879 (Sullivan, Tennessee, 1880 US census)

Lizzie Pervert
Born *c.*1868; married Horace Hayes, Redfield,
New York, USA, 1 October 1901
Lizzie Pervert was the daughter of Max Pervert.

Trannie Pickup
(Female) Born Portsmouth, Hampshire, *c.*1853
(Grays, Essex, 1901 England census)

Hyman Pleasure
Born New York, USA, 31 May 1908; died Orangeburg, New York,
USA, June 1982

Elizabeth Pokeme
Born *c.*1880 (Calumet, Michigan, 1930 US census)

Nicolaus Porn
Married Elisabetha Krones, Alflen, Prussia, 31 August 1858

Anita Porno
Born Santa Fe, *c.*1891 (Santa Fe, 1895 Argentina census)

Trinidad Porno
Baptized El Garrario, Santiago, Chile, 1 April 1842

Wolf Porno
Born Hungary, *c.*1870; passenger on *Wieland,* Hamburg, Germany–New York, USA, arrived 12 July 1888

Dick Pounder
Born Sculcoates, Yorkshire, 1903

Fanny Pounder
Born Manchester, Lancashire, 1879

Ada Prick
Died Winnebago, Wisconsin, USA, 19 July 1886

Henrietta Prick
Born Germany, *c.*1855 (Camden, Missouri, 1910 US census)

Suca Prick
Born Reed, Suffolk, *c.*1753

Lord Prickup
Born Pemberton, Lancashire, *c.*1856 (Accrington, Lancashire, 1901 England census)

Dick Prickwell
Baptized St Botolph without Aldgate, London, 16 December 1669

Lovie Prickwell
Born Virginia, USA, 7 August 1887

Ophelia Pubes
Born Louisiana, *c.*1825 (Assumption, Louisiana, 1870 US census)

Pulls It Out
(Male) Born *c.*1892 (South Dakota, 1894 US Indian census)

Ernest Pumper
Born Isle of Sheppey, Kent, *c.*1882 (Faversham, Kent, 1901 England census)

Ophelia Pusey
Born Illinois, *c.*1866 (Condit, Champaign, Illinois, 1870 USA census)

Justin Pussy
Married Marie Salleron, Paris, France, 2 May 1821

Semen Rapoport
Born Russia, *c.*1859
(Edmonton, Middlesex, 1911 England census)

E. Rect
Born Iowa, *c.*1910 (Shenandoah, Iowa, 1930 US census)

Bonk Register
(Male) Born Florida, 1862 (Hamilton, Florida, 1880 US census)

Randy Rimmer
Born 6 October 1962; died Iredell, North Carolina, USA,
February 1986

George Rimming
Born Hampshire, *c.*1826
(Upham, Hampshire, 1841 England census)

William Horny Robinson
Born Hull, Yorkshire, *c.*1847 (Hull, 1901 England census)

Kunt Rubbing
Born Sweden, *c.*1877
(Westmoreland, Pennsylvania, 1910 US census)

Rudolph Rumplick
Born New York, 1889 (Islip, New York, 1900 US census)

Semen Sacks
Born Illinois, *c.*1862 (Elbe, Washington, 1930 US census)

Emma Manuel Screw
Baptized St John, Wakefield, Yorkshire, 11 January 1821

Ophelia Seaman
Born New York, *c.*1833 (Reading, New York, 1860 US census)

Ani Semen
Married Peno Penoff, York, Ontario, Canada,
6 October 1913

Ben Semen

Born Gorleston, Norfolk, *c*.1890 (Gorleston, 1911 England census)
*As recorded in the 1911 census, the Semen family consisted of
Ben, a carter by trade, his wife of ten months, Florence Semen,
and their seven-month-old daughter Gertrude Semen.*

Isaac Semen

Married Caroline E. Hogan, St Clair, Illinois, USA, 19 January 1843

Goulia Semenoff

(Male) Born Russia, *c*.1904 (Islington, London, 1911 England census)
*In addition to their son Goulia, the Semenoff family comprised
Russian architect Wladimiz, his wife Abetina and daughters
Swetia and Olga.*

Ah Sex

(Male) Born China, *c*.1841 (Pima, Arizona, 1880 US census)

Earl E. Sex

Born 22 September 1919; died Licking, Ohio, USA, 19 March 2003

Maria Pringle Sex

Baptized St Bride's Fleet Street, London, 30 July 1831

Louis B. Sexfinger

Born Poland, 6 January 1885; died Los Angeles, California,
USA, 27 January 1960

Lobias Sexhouse

(Male) Born *c*.1810 (Plain, Stark, Ohio, 1870 US census)

Oral Sexton

Born Illinois, *c*.1904
(Granite City, Madison, Illinois, 1930 US census)

Willy Shafting

Married Margaret Dawkins, Hildersham, Cambridgeshire,
4 August 1712

Ernest Shag

Born Germany, *c*.1905
(Cheyenne, Laramie, Wyoming, 1920 US census)

Catherine Shagger
Daughter of Andrew and Catherine Shagger, born 2 August 1814;
baptized Trichinopoly, Tamil Nadu, India, 7 August 1814

Kitty Shagger
Born New Jersey 1879 (Newark, New Jersey, 1900 US census)

Virgena Shagger
Born Norway, *c.*1865 (Clay, Dakota Territory, 1880 US census)

John Shaghard
Born Scotland, 1883
(Victoria, British Columbia, 1911 Canada census)

Kurt Roger Shagme
Born Norway, *c.*1925; passenger on *Stavangerfjord*, Oslo,
Norway–New York, USA, arrived 22 April 1947

Susanna Shags
Born Essex, *c.*1821 (Little Wakering, Essex, 1841 England census)
Her daughter, born c.1840, had the same name.

Hanorah Shagwell
Born Shenandoah, Virginia, USA, 1830; married Michael Flynn,
Shenandoah, USA, 27 April 1856

Eric Shon
Born California, USA, 1990

Caroline Fuckson Shucksmith
Born Lincoln, *c.*1882
(Grimsby, Lincolnshire, 1911 England census)

Hannah Quick Shugg
Born Penzance, Cornwall, 1852

Lottie Sperm
Born *c.*1904 (Rankin, Mississippi, 1930 US census)

Lottie Spunk
Born Germany, 1886 (Queens, New York, 1900 US census)

Amelia Ann Spurting
Baptized St Paul's, Deptford, Kent, 5 March 1845

Anna Squirts
Born *c.*1893 (Charleston, West Virginia, 1930 US census)

Semion Staines
(Male) Born Maldon, Essex, *c.*1863
(Maldon, 1871 England census)

Dick Stiff
Born St Luke, Middlesex, 1846

Clinton Stiffy
Born Nebraska, *c.*1880 (Union, Butler, Nebraska, 1880 US census)

Dick Stillhard
Born 3 July 1913; died Rochester, New York,
USA, 11 November 1993

Fanny Stuffer
Born Ohio, 1893 (Dayton, Ohio, 1900 US census)

Elizabeth Suckcock
Born *c.*1816 (Aston, Birmingham, 1841 England census)

Dick Sucker
Born Minnesota, *c.*1894 (Nicollet, Minnesota, 1910 US census)

Willy Sucker
Born Germany, *c.*1907; crew on *Hansa*, Hamburg,
Germany–New York, USA, arrived 2 July 1936

Sully Suckhole
(Male) Born St Petersburg, Russia, *c.*1868
(Whitechapel, London, 1891 England census)

Mary Cox Suckling
Born Hanworth, Middlesex, *c.*1844
(Kidbrooke, Kent, 1851 England census)

Flora Suckoff
Married John Fisher, Cuyahoga, Ohio, USA, 12 November 1890

Sucks As He Walks
Born *c.*1893 (South Dakota, 1895 US Indian census)

Lulu Suckup
Born Austria, 1893 (Upper Tyrone, Pennsylvania, 1900 US census)

Willy Suckwell
Baptized Asthall, Oxfordshire, 17 June 1838

Semen Suk
Born Grodno, Russia, *c.*1882; passenger on *Haverford*, Liverpool,
England–Philadelphia, Pennsylvania, USA, arrived 17 June 1907

Amaziah Swallow
Married Asenath Cumings, Dunstable, Massachusetts, USA,
18 January 1810

Pansye Swallows
Born 4 November 1909; died Fort Lauderdale, Florida, USA,
14 January 2001

Dick Swinger
Born Texas, *c.*1895 (Harris, Texas, 1930 US census)

Fanny Swinger
Born Tennessee, 1835 (Giles, Tennessee, 1900 US census)

Rolena Throbs
Born 11 March 1934; died Gary, Indiana, USA, 18 December 2004

Dick Thrust
Goudhurst, Kent, 1598 (Will)

Dick Tickler
Baptized Sutton le Marsh, Lincolnshire, 11 May 1707

Fanny Tickler
Born Withern, Lincolnshire, *c.*1859
(Grimsby, Lincolnshire, 1881 England census)

Phil A. Tio
Born *c.*1862; married William P. Rideau, New Orleans,
Louisiana, USA, 12 November 1883
*She was called Philomene A. Tio, but was known to her
intimate friends as 'Phil'.*

Kate *née* Trembler
Married William Jones, Chorlton, Lancashire, 1892

Fucker Tucker
Born Hastings, Ontario, Canada, 7 August 1901

Semen Tugwell
Born Westonbirt, Gloucestershire, *c.*1794 (Frampton Cotterell,
Gloucestershire, 1861 England census)

Jennet Twiceaday
Married Edward Fell, Bolton-le-Sands, Lancashire,
27 September 1685

Peter Upass
Born Mexico, *c.*1866 (Jackson, Louisiana, 1910 US census)

Martha Uphard
Born Eau Claire, Wisconsin, USA, 12 January 1899

Dick Upright
Born Exeter, Devon, 1862

Joanna Street Walker
Born 14 November 1884; died Orange, Florida, USA,
8 November 1972

Dildo Arthur Waller
Born Ohio, *c.*1915 (Cuyahoga, Ohio, 1920 US census)

Fuck Wang
Born China, 1862
(Lewiston City, Nez Perce, Idaho, 1900 US census)

Dick Well
Born Wisconsin, *c.*1897 (Holland, Wisconsin, 1920 US census)

Henrietta Willy
Born New York, *c.*1832 (New York, 1850 US census)

Ophelia Willy
Born Mississippi, *c.*1902 (Alcorn, Mississippi, 1920 US census)

Man Suck You
Born *c.*1882; crew on *America Maru*, Kobe, Japan–San Francisco,
USA, arrived 9 October 1904

Fuk Yu
Born China, *c.*1852
(Vancouver, British Columbia, 1901 Canada census)

Yutaka Yufuku
Married Nevada, USA, 1966

IZZY GAY?

In the interests of sexual equality, this section of the book presents a selection of gay, lesbian and bisexual names. This is not to suggest that any of these individuals engaged in man-on-man or girl-on-girl action and, of course, the humour in many cases results from linguistic change. Being known by a name such as Gay Bender in Alabama in the 1930s, for example, would probably not have raised as much as a smirk.

Dick Ass
Born Kolberg, Prussia, 23 November 1881

Lesbos Auguste
Born France, *c.*1891; passenger on *Czar*, Brest,
France–New York, USA, arrived 9 November 1918

Gay Barr
(Male) Born Illinois, *c.*1893
(Lake Creek, Williamson, Illinois, 1910 US census)

Les Bean
Born Iowa, *c.*1864 (Lone Oak, Missouri, 1930 US census)

Cowboy Begay
Born 15 July 1904; died Kykotsmovi Village, Arizona, USA, July 1981

Les Behan
Born Iowa, *c.*1887 (Mohall, North Dakota, 1930 US census)

Fanny Bender
Married Woolf Bagel, City of London, 1913

Gay Bender
(Male) Born Alabama, *c.*1861
(Georgiana, Alabama, 1930 US census)

Liz Bian
Born Maryland, *c.*1849 (Baltimore, Maryland, 1880 US census)

Fanny Biggadyke
Baptized Whaplode, Lincolnshire, 24 May 1744

Edward Biggerdyke
Buried Howden, Yorkshire, 28 July 1660

Gay Bird
Born Indiana, *c.*1888 (Wabash, Indiana, 1930 US census)

Ruth Bisex
Married Joseph Hamblyn, Kilmersdon, Somerset, 25 July 1742

Ellen Bothways
Born Wisbech, Cambridgeshire, 1848

Gay Boy
(Male) Born China, *c*.1891
(Kootenay, British Columbia, 1911 Canada census)

Nancy Boy
Born Illinois, *c*.1819 (Sebastian, Arkansas, 1860 US census)

Nancy Boys
Born Brighton, Sussex, *c*.1842 (Brighton, 1871 England census)

Robert Bumming Browne
Born Scotland, *c*.1880 (Newington, London, 1901 England census)

Erasmus Bugger
Born North Shields, Northumberland, *c*.1876
(Hackney, London, 1901 England census)

Pleasant Bugger
Born Arkansas, *c*.1910 (Redland, Arkansas, 1920 US census)

Will Bumass
Born Birmingham, Warwickshire, *c.*1892
(Birmingham, 1901 England census)

Charles Bumboy
Born Lexden, Essex, 1844

Melchior Bumhold
Born Switzerland, *c.*1863; passenger on *Canada*, Le Havre,
France–New York, USA, arrived 5 March 1885

Nancy Bummer
Born Rhode Island, *c.*1800
(Hounsfield, New York, 1900 US census)

Dick Bumming
Born Clam Union, Missaukee, Michigan, USA, 9 March 1894

May Bumwell
Born Indiana, *c.*1843 (Milford, Nebraska, 1870 US census)

Bugger Cheeks
(Male) Born Georgia, *c.*1891 (Raiford, Georgia, 1910 US census)

H. Gay Cock
Born *c.*1862; immigrant on *Buninyong* to Melbourne,
Australia, arrived 11 March 1888

Gay Coffin
(Male) Born Vermont, *c.*1899
(Washington, Vermont, 1910 US census)

Dick Cottage
Baptized St George, Barbados, 20 October 1824

Gay Day
Born Virginia, *c.*1859 (Richmond, Virginia, 1870 US census)

Gay Dick
Born New Brunswick, *c.*1882
(New Brunswick, 1891 Canada census)

Charles Biggin Dyke
Married Wincanton, Somerset, 1848

Dorcas Wanklin Dyke
Born Gloucester, 1843

Fanny Dyke
Born West Virginia, 1874 (Piedmont, West Virginia, 1900 US census)

Harry Dyke
Born Germany, *c.*1883 (Sausalito, California, 1910 US census)

Queenie Dyke
Born Bath, Somerset, 1911

Randy Dyke
Born Alderbury, Wiltshire, 1886

Rhoda Dyke
Born New York, *c.*1827 (Amity, New York, 1850 US census)

Wilfred Titanic Dyke
Born 1912; died Chorley, Lancashire, 1985

Buell Dykes
(Male) Born Oklahoma, 11 May 1903
(Waconda, Oklahoma, 1910 US census)

Dorphus Fagg
Born c.1913 (Bazaar, Chase, Kansas, 1930 US census)

Valentine Faggott
Born North Carolina, 1750
(Mecklenburg, North Carolina, 1790 US census)

Berndt Fisting
Married Elisabeth Heggemans, Emsdetten, Prussia, 27 April 1681

Lesbia Fox
Born Pennsylvania, c.1838
(Kalamazoo, Michigan, 1860 US census)

Brighton Gay
Married Helston, Cornwall, 1881

Gladys Gay
Born Bedwelty, Monmouthshire, 1898

Ima Gay
Born Mississippi, c.1872 (Moscow, Mississippi, 1900 US census)

Isabel More Gay
Born USA, c.1897; passenger on Pan Am flight, Rio de Janeiro,
Brazil–New York, USA, 15 April 1948

Izzy Gay
Born 12 May 1897; died Inverell, New South Wales, Australia,
3 October 1980

Less Gay
Born c.1897 (Gulf, Florida, 1945 Florida state census)

Pansy Gay
Born Iowa, USA, 20 February 1901; died San Francisco,
California, USA, 8 May 1957

Queen Gay
Born Georgia, *c.*1882 (Butts, Georgia, 1910 US census)

Shag Gay
(Female) Born *c.*1882
(San Carlos, Arizona, 1904 US Indian census)

Guiseppe Gaybeard
Shoemaker, Elizabeth, New Jersey, USA
(1883–91 New Jersey directories)

Konstons Gaydick
Born Russia, *c.*1879; passenger on *Pennsylvania*, Hamburg,
Germany–New York, USA, arrived 10 May 1901

Dingus Gayheart
Born 22 May 1886; died Jefferson, Kentucky, USA,
10 August 1973

Oscar Gaylard
Born Plymouth, Devon, 1884

Sodom Hardin
Born Alabama, *c.*1842
(Wayne, Tennessee, 1860 US census)

Gay Head
(Male) Born Iowa, 1890 (Reading, Iowa, 1900 US census)

Camp Henry
Born Islington, London, *c.*1840 (Islington, 1901 England census)

John Knobs Henry
Born Cookstown, Ireland, *c.*1837
(Greenwich, Kent, 1881 England census)

Ole Homo
Born Norway, 1867
(White, South Dakota, 1900 US census)

Gay Hooker
Born New York, *c.*1879
(Carrollton, New York, 1880 US census)

Annie Gayman Hoover
Born Markham, Ontario, Canada, 1854;
died Markham, Ontario, Canada, 27 November 1915

Dick Inman
Born Manchester, *c.*1872 (Chorlton, Lancashire, 1891 census)

Catherine Ladyboyse
Born Germany, *c.*1836
(Pomfret, Chautauqua, New York, 1850 US census)

Raspberry Gay Lay
Born Florida, *c.*1869 (Amite, Mississippi, 1870 US census)

Humberto Lesbia
Born Italy, 1888; married Margarita Lesbia, Aldesa,
Córdoba, Argentina, 1911

Angel Lesbian
Son of Luis M. Lesbian; baptized Santa Veracruz, Guerrero Sureste,
Mexico, 25 December 1898

Sapho Jane Lesbini
Born France, *c.*1874 (Islington, London, 1911 England census)

Ben A. Lesbo
Born 17 February 1927; died Elko, Nevada, USA, 18 May 1994

Lula Lesbo
Married Jesse Eugene Prothers, Hamilton, Caldwell, Missouri,
USA, 25 December 1921

Gay Lust
Born 5 January 1909; died Spokane, Washington, USA,
9 March 1995

Bisexter McCauley
Born Kentucky, *c.*1895 (Louisville, Kentucky, 1930 US census)

Nancy McQueer
Born USA, *c.*1874 (Bothwell, Ontario, 1891 Canada census)

Gay Man
Born *c.*1916 (Ravenna, Michigan, 1930 US census)

Peter Mansuck
Born New York, 1879 (First World War draft registration)

Oscar Bumboy Millard
Born Pennsylvania, *c.*1909
(Northumberland, Pennsylvania, 1910 US census)

Gay Ness
(Male) Born *c.*1902 (Aux Sable, Grundy, Illinois, 1930 US census)

Fanny Sappho Pogson
Born Christchurch, Hampshire, 1886

Minor Poof
Born Virginia, *c.*1910 (Chester, Pennsylvania, 1920 US census)

Phillip Poofy
Born Italy, *c.*1860 (Bucks, Pennsylvania, 1910 US census)

Francesco Poove
Born Italy, *c.*1883; passenger on *Florida*, Naples, Italy–New York,
USA, arrived 23 March 1906

Gay Pope
(Male) Born Missouri, *c.*1880
(Nashville, Missouri, 1920 US census)

Gay Power
(Female) Resident of Kalgoorlie, Western Australia, 1906
(1901–36 Australian electoral rolls)

Gay Pride
Born 16 April 1917; died Wandsworth, London, May 2003

Gay Priest
Born Ohio, *c.*1902 (Bridgewater, Ohio, 1920 US census)

Gay Queen
Born West Virginia, *c.*1906
(Salt Lick, West Virginia, 1910 US census)

Oscar Queer
Born Pennsylvania, *c.*1885 (Derry, Pennsylvania, 1910 US census)

Joseph Man Rear
Baptized Heckington, Lincolnshire, 27 May 1820

William Shirtlift
Born Rotherham, Yorkshire, 1859

Dick Sodom
Baptized Coseley in Sedgley, Staffordshire, 4 July 1836

Thomas Sodomy
Born Ontario, *c.*1837 (Winchester, Ontario, 1871 Canada census)

Zuzana Strapon
Born Czechoslovakia, *c.*1894; passenger on *Majestic*, Cherbourg,
France–Boston, Massachusetts, USA, arrived 1 August 1923

Willie Vaseline
Born Illinois, 1896 (Chicago, Illinois, 1900 US census)

Baxter Wall
Born Mississippi, *c.*1898 (West Carroll, Louisiana, 1930 US census)

Dick Woofter
Born Nottinghamshire, *c.*1906 (Nottingham, 1841 England census)

Gay Woofter
Born West Virginia, *c.*1902
(Freemans Creek, West Virginia, 1910 US census

A CELEBRATION OF MASTURBATION

While the parental inflicting of many of the names in this book could be regarded as a form of abuse, those that follow contain implications of self-abuse.

Celia Wankoff Adelman
Born 14 November 1898; died Dade, Florida, USA, 15 October 1970

W. Ank
(Male) Born Southwark, London, c.1816
(Gravesend, Kent, 1851 England census)

W. Anker
(Male) Baptized Wonersh, Surrey, 28 July 1877

George W. Ankers
Born Prescot, Lancashire, 1911

Wanker Baker
Born Missouri, c.1873
(Grand Pass, Saline, Missouri, 1880 US census)

Master Bates
Born Pulaski, Kentucky, USA, 16 December 1859

Dick Beater
Born Norwich, Norfolk, c.1835
(Wisbech, Norfolk, 1851 England census)
At the time of the census, young Dick Beater was a
sixteen-year-old prisoner in Wisbech jail.

Fanny Frigger
Died Beckley, Northiam, Sussex, 17 March 1849

Wanka Hamburger
Born Városlöd, Hungary, c.1912; passenger on *Lapland*, Antwerp,
Belgium–New York, USA, arrived 14 August 1921

Wank Hardy
Born Idle, Yorkshire, c.1892 (Idle, 1901 England census)

Fanny Jackoff
Born c.1919 (New York, 1930 US census)

Hyman Jackoff
Born Pennsylvania, c.1907 (Philadelphia, 1910 US census)

Zanch Jerkoff
Born c.1872 (Bucks, Pennsylvania, 1920 US census)

Anna Jerkoffsky
Born Rhode Island, USA, 29 September 1885

Wan Kerr
(Male) Born Ontario, c.1892 (Bothwell, Ontario, 1891 Canada census)

Juan King
Born Mississippi, c.1904 (Franklin, Mississippi, 1920 US census)

Wan King
(Male) Born Delaware, c.1825 (Wilson, Illinois, 1860 US census)

Wang King
Born 15 October 1904; died New York, USA, 18 April 2001

Dick Massage
Born 25 September 1737; baptized St Martin Vintry, London,
9 October 1737

Roman Mastabata

Born Russia, *c.*1880 (Youngstown, Ohio, 1920 US census)

Jack Off
Born *c.*1883
(Livonia, North Dakota, USA, 1925 North Dakota census)

Plays With Himself
Born Montana, *c.*1873 (Big Horn, Montana, 1920 US census)

Wackoff Roe
Resident of Monmouth, New Jersey, USA
(1895 New Jersey census)

Vaseline Rogers
Born Arkansas, 1893 (Caddo, Arkansas, 1900 US census)

Dick Rubber
Passenger on *City of Adelaide*, Melbourne–Sydney,
Australia, arrived 14 March 1882

Ophelia Self
Born Louisiana, 1873 (Vernon, Louisiana, 1900 US census)

Dick Stroker
Born *c.*1926 (Oak Park, Illinois, 1930 US census)

Jackoff Thurnbeck
Born Hungary, 1875 (Columbus, Minnesota, 1900 US census)

Willie Tissue
Born Georgia, *c.*1903 (Lee, Georgia, 1910 US census)

Unice Tosser
Born Canada, *c.*1820 (Monmouth, Iowa, 1880 US census)

Willy Tosser
Born Glasgow, Scotland, *c.*1827
(Barony, Lanarkshire, 1851 Scotland census)

Nikola Tossoff
(Male) Born Serbia, *c.*1897; passenger on *Oceanic*, Southampton,
England–New York, USA, arrived 30 April 1914

Dick Wacker
Born Illinois, *c.*1901 (Rosendale, Minnesota, 1910 US census)

Max Wackoff
Born Russia, *c.*1858 (Bronx, New York, 1920 US census)

Ernest Wank
Born Islington, London, *c.*1855
(Streatham, London, 1911 England census)
*At the time of the 1911 census, Ernest Wank was an accountant,
his son Douglas Wank a stockbroker, his daughters Marjorie and
Muriel Wank both clerks, while eighteen-year-old daughter
Eleanor Wank had 'no occupation'.*

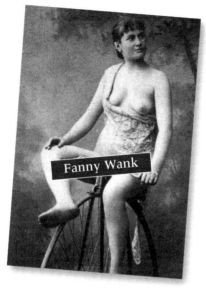

Fanny Wank

Born Germany, *c.*1839 (New York, 1870 US census)

Hank Wank
Born Pennsylvania, *c.*1817 (Forks, Pennsylvania, 1850 US census)

Hans Wank
Married Barbara Wyrt, Zürich, Switzerland, 14 March 1585

Max Wank
Born France, *c.*1863; passenger on *Kaiser Wilhelm der Grosse*, Cherbourg, France–New York, USA, arrived 7 June 1906

May Wank
Born Kirkee, India, *c.*1886
(Charlton, London, 1901 England census)

Willie Harriet Wank
Born Leytonstone, Essex, *c.*1868
(Wanstead, Essex, 1871 England census)
To compound the embarrassment of his surname, Willie Wank received his mother's first name as his middle name.

Manley Wanka
Born *c.*1911 (Erie, New York, 1920 US census)

Emma Wanker
Born Ontario, 1888 (Welland, Ontario, 1911 Canada census)

Max Wanker
Born Germany, 1878 (Chicago, Illinois, 1900 US census)

Minnie Wanker
Born Iowa, *c.*1883 (Keya Paha, Nebraska, 1910 US census)

Urban Wanker
Born 24 February 1892; died Milwaukee, Wisconsin, USA,
September 1977

Hardin Wankin
Born Bremen, Germany, *c.*1814
(Warren, Minnesota, 1870 US census)

Willie Wanking
Born *c.*1876 (Freshwater, Isle of Wight, 1911 England census)

Minnie Wankoff
Born Russia, *c.*1885 (New York, 1920 US census)

Willy Wankoff
Born New York, 1 June 1917 (Bronx, New York, 1930 US census)

Bessie Wankwell
Born England, *c.*1849; passenger on *Wisconsin*, Liverpool,
England–New York, USA, arrived 3 April 1871

U. BASTARD AND OTHER INSULTING NAMES

Imagine if every time you were asked your name you had to reply 'Dick Head' or 'Bitch' – you'd probably change it. The fact that these people did not do so is, I think, testament to their strength of character.

Edmund Rodney Pollexen Bastard
Died Isle of Wight, Hampshire, 1856

Ellen U. Bastard
Born Cley next the Sea, Norfolk, 1866

A. Bitch
Married Racine, Wisconsin, USA, 8 April 1880

Christ Bogoff
Born Macedonia, c.1885 (Akron, Ohio, 1930 US census)

Dick Brain
Born Stoke-on-Trent, Staffordshire, 1871

Sophia Crappy
Baptized Maker, Cornwall, 17 January 1802

U. Cunte
(Male) Born Nova Scotia, Canada
(Chicago, Illinois, 1920 US census)

Ura Dick
(Female) Born 17 February 1890; died New York, USA, 1976
Ura was the mother of Rubin Dick.

John Dickshit
Born Pennsylvania, *c.*1866 (Earl, Pennsylvania, 1880 US census)

Dick Face
Baptized Ridgmont, Bedfordshire, 14 July 1551

Elizabeth Forkoff
Born Ohio, 1862 (Cincinnati, Ohio, 1880 US census)

You Fuck
Born Canton, China, *c.*1852
(Marysville, California, 1880 US census)

Angel P. Fukoff
Born Bulgaria, *c.*1880; passenger on *Breslau*, Bremen,
Germany–Baltimore, USA, arrived June 1907

Louisa Greatbitch
Born Longton, Staffordshire, *c.*1816
(Longton, 1861 England census)

Fanny Harlot
Born Ore, Sussex, *c.*1888 (Ore, 1891 England census)

Dick Head
Born Texas, *c.*1895 (Maxwell, Oklahoma, 1910 US census)

Fat Ho
Born Hawaii, *c.*1865 (Honolulu, Hawaii, 1910 US census)

Alured Hoar
Born Brimfield, Massachusetts, USA, 29 January 1796
In 1838, the entire Hoar family legally changed their surname to Homer.

Kissy Hoare
Born London, *c.*1879 (Shanklin, Isle of Wight, 1901 England census)

Ima Hore
Born *c.*1896 (Durham, North Carolina, 1930 US census)

Pervert King
Born Texas, *c.*1916 (Runge, Texas, 1920 US census)

Martha Manky
Married William Waterhouse, Calverley, Yorkshire,
8 February 1798

Fanny Minger
Born South Carolina, *c.*1855
(Fairfield, South Carolina, 1870 US census)

Fuckie Offshlay
(Female) Born Russia, *c.*1890 (New York, 1910 US census)

Dick Perve
Born Germany, *c.*1876 (Rock Island, Illinois, 1930 US census)

Albert Ponce
Born Birmingham, Warwickshire, *c.*1882
(Solihull, Warwickshire, 1891 England census)

Harlot Price
(Male) Born Shropshire, *c.*1832
(Clun, Shropshire, 1841 England census)

Nimrod Shitehead
Born Kentucky, *c.*1838 (Harrison, Kentucky, 1910 US census)
The Shitehead household consisted of twins Florence and Clarence Shitehead (born c.*1890) and daughter-in-law Emma Shitehead (born* c.*1882).*

Eunice Singletart
Born Salisbury, Massachusetts, USA, 7 January 1641

Ada Slag
Born St Peter Port, Guernsey, Channel Islands, *c.*1870
(Willesden, Middlesex, 1901 England census)

Salome Slapper
Born Chipping Sodbury,
Gloucestershire, 1891

Sisi Slapper
Born St George's, London, *c.*1906
(Mile End, London, 1911
England census)

Fanny Slattern
Born South Carolina, *c.*1869
(Grove, Greenville, South Carolina,
1870 US census)

Rowland R. Slicker
Born 10 December 1929;
died Dallas, Texas, USA,
13 March 1996

A. Lotta Slut
Born Vaasa, Finland,
9 February 1827

Jessie Slut
Born Wimbledon, Surrey, *c.*1889
(St George, London, 1911
England census)
*At the time of the 1911 census, Ms
Slut was a housemaid in the Eaton
Square home of barrister John
Hutton Balfour Browne, KC.*

Magdalena Slutty
Married Frederick Beck, Columbiana, Ohio, USA,
15 May 1834

Minnie Sodoff
Born Michigan, *c.*1867
(Climax, Kalamazoo, Michigan, 1880 US census)

Nancy Strumpet
Married John Palmore, Floyd, Georgia, USA, 28 June 1891

Craven Tart
Born North Carolina, *c.*1917
(Newton Grove, Sampson, North Carolina, 1920 US census)

Sydney Shitehead Thompson
Born Leeds, Yorkshire, *c.*1900 (Leeds, 1901 England census)

Silly Trollope
(Female) Born Doncaster, Yorkshire, *c.*1894
(Doncaster, 1901 England census)

Bestial L. Ushitaker
Born England, 1904
(Lisgar, Manitoba, 1911 Canada census)

Alice Whore
Married Francis Smyth, Brinklow, Warwickshire,
17 January 1604

Lulu Whore
Born Texas, *c.*1886 (Kaufman, Texas, 1910 US census)

Poncy Windhorn
Born Alabama, *c.*1899
(Cross Roads, Pike, Alabama, 1930 US census)

A NASTY DOSE

Most of the names in this book are bad enough, but having the double indignity of a name that is not only vulgar, but also connotes some unpleasant disease, is both cruel and unusual.

Puss Aids
Born Georgia, *c.*1844 (Bibb, Georgia, 1880 US census)
Mrs Aids, a seamstress, shared her home with a thirteen-year-old servant called Fannie Dikes.

Sore Ass
Born Russia, *c.*1897; passenger on *Russia*, Libau, Latvia–New York, USA, arrived 9 March 1914

Jean Ballache
Born France, *c.*1870
(St Savour, Jersey, 1891 Channel Islands census)

Willy Ballitch
Born *c.*1909 (Mifflin, Ohio, 1930 US census)

Hurse Bumache
Born France, *c.*1888 (St Boniface Town, Manitoba, Canada, 1906 Manitoba, Saskatchewan and Alberta census)

Georgia W. Bunpain
Born Michigan, *c.*1883 (Battle Creek, Michigan, 1920 US census)

Thrush Burns
(Female) Born Ireland, *c.*1845
(Boston, Massachusetts, 1880 US census)

Nicolas Chancre
Born Merviller, France, 8 August 1751

Charity Clap
Baptized Branscombe, Devon, 11 June 1643

Dick Clap
Married Mary Blake, Boston, Massachusetts, USA, 26 September 1807

Increase Clap
Born Dorchester, Dorset, *c*.1625

Mora Cockburn
Born St Marylebone, London, *c*.1894
(Paddington, London, 1901 England census)

Dick Crabs
Born St Germans, Cornwall, 1853

Sore Fukin
(Female) Born *c*.1859; passenger on *Vaderland*, Antwerp,
Belgium–New York, USA, arrived 1 June 1904

Dick Gleet
Baptized Wistanstow, Shropshire, 14 October 1683
Gleet, from the Latin glittus, *meaning sticky, is used to describe
the discharge associated with a sexually transmitted disease;
having it as a surname seems harsh punishment indeed.*

Ransom Herpes
(Male) Born Kentucky, *c*.1854 (Shelby, Tennessee, 1880 US census)

Dick Itchcock
Born Huntingdonshire, *c*.1856
(Basford, Nottinghamshire, 1881 England census)

Bloody Knob
Born *c*.1879 (Fresno, California, 1860 US census)

Dick Lumpy
Born *c*.1859 (Islington, London, 1881 England census)

Rector Piles
Born Virginia, *c*.1833 (Hampshire, Virginia, 1850 US census)

Fanny Pong
Born Mansell Gamage, Herefordshire, *c*.1855
(Mansell Gamage, 1861 England census)

Nancy Pox
Married George W. Monday, Fayette, Georgia, USA,
28 December 1846

Dick Rash
Born Chesterton, Cambridgeshire, 1872

Benedict Rimstinger
Married Ursula Sumser, Herdern, Germany, 29 May 1817

Emma Royds
Resident of Macquarie, New South Wales, 1930
(1901–36 Australian electoral rolls)

Anal Saw
Born Lewisham, London, 1913

Fannie Scratcher
Born Switzerland, 1844 (West Cleveland, Ohio, 1880 US census)

Valentine Soranus
Born Santo Domingo, Dominican Republic, *c.*1898
(Brooklyn, New York, 1920 US census)

Dolores Herpes Unclan
Born Spain, *c.*1880; passenger on *Saxonia*, Liverpool,
England–Boston, Massachusetts, USA, arrived 24 May 1906

Signa Veedee
(Female) Born Sweden, 1870 (New York, 1900 US census)

Dick Wart
Born Northamptonshire, *c.*1811
(Silverstone, Northamptonshire, 1841 England census)

Poxy Wolf
Born New York, *c.*1829 (Albany, New York, 1850 census)

UNMITIGATED FILTH

Horace's phrase quoted in Samuel Butler's *The Way of All Flesh*, *'delicta majorum immeritus lues'*, which means 'innocent heirs will pay for the crimes of their ancestors', is translated in a schoolboy howler as 'the delights of our ancestors were unmitigated filth' – and well they might have been, if some of them bore such names.

Angeline Shit Gun
Born *c.*1879 (Wyoming, 1897 US Indian census)

Shit E. Brown
Born Georgia, *c.*1918 (Elko, Georgia, 1920 US census)

Turdy Brown
Born Iowa, 1879 (Blaine, Butte, South Dakota, 1900 US census)

Buffalo Shit
(Female) Born *c.*1836 (Dakota Territory, 1886 US Indian census)

Bull That Shits Loose
(Female) Born *c.*1826 (Dakota Territory, 1888 US Indian census)

Shitty Bunn
(Male) Born North Carolina, *c.*1869
(Springfield, North Carolina, 1870 US census)

Farting Clack
Born London, *c.*1863 (Walthamstow, Essex, 1871 England census)

Oleveiah Cockshit
Born Great Harne, Lancashire, *c.*1836
(Accrington, Lancashire, 1861 England census)

Harry Crap
Born Bruton, Buckinghamshire, *c.*1846
(Oxford, 1891 England census)

Love Crapping
Married Edward Addicot, Brixham, Devon, 17 February 1712

Joshua Crapwell
Born England, *c.*1866; passenger on *Chester*, Southampton,
England–New York, USA, arrived 20 June 1893

John Dickshit
Born Pennsylvania, *c.*1866 (Earl, Pennsylvania, 1880 US census)

Dog Urine
Born np, nd (Wyoming, 1885 US Indian census)

I. Doshit
(Female) Born Louisiana, *c.*1889
(New Orleans, Louisiana, 1910 US census)

Latrine Dubois
Born Lewisham, London, *c.*1890
(Lewisham, 1891 England census)

Dinah Dump
Born Whitechapel, London, 1897

Godfrey Fartarsie
Born Québec, Canada, *c.*1879 Selkirk, Manitoba, Canada
(1906 Manitoba, Saskatchewan and Alberta census)

Ivan Farting Haarburger
Born *c.*1869; passenger on *Windsor Castle*, Durban,
South Africa–Southampton, England, arrived 30 May 1927

Urinal Jones
(Female) Born Llanllwni, Carmarthenshire, Wales, *c.*1889
(Llanllwni, 1891 Wales census)

Anal Leak
(Male) Married Mildred Inness, Royal Oak, Wayne, Michigan,
USA, 5 August 1923

Fanny May Leak
Born Poplar, London, 1886

Urine Mann
Born Kentucky, 1900 (Spring Fork, Kentucky, 1900 US census)

Will Passwater
Born New Jersey, *c.*1901 (Camden, New Jersey, 1910 US census)

Isabella Peedon
Married Manchester, Lancashire, 1840

Pissed In The Road
(Female) Born 1844 (Dakota, 1887 US Indian census)

Fanny Pisser
Born New York, *c.*1856 (New York, 1860 US census)

Doshit Royster
(Female) Born Missouri, *c.*1897
(Gasconade, Missouri, 1920 US census)

Jack Schitz
Born Austria, 28 September 1888
(Dane, Wisconsin, USA, First World War draft registration)

Ah Shit
Born China, 1844 (Granite, Grant, Oregon, 1880 US census)

Minnie Shit
Born Prussia, *c.*1805 (Farmington, Wisconsin, 1880 US census)

Shit Bird
Born *c.*1893 (Montana, 1895 US Indian census)

Daisy Shite
Born Gravesend, Kent, *c.*1893
(Basingstoke, Hampshire, 1911 England census)

Ethel May Shitehouse
Born Coventry, Warwickshire, *c.*1892
(Wolverhampton, Staffordshire, 1911 England census)

George Melbourn Shithard
Born Camberwell, London, *c.*1896
(Lambeth, London, 1911 England census)

Sophia Shithouse
Born Germany, *c.*1823 (Poland, Mahoning, Ohio, 1850 US census)

Maria Shitson
Born Launceston, Cornwall, *c.*1812
(Launceston, 1851 England census)

Arthur Shitter
Born Bury St Edmunds, Suffolk, *c.*1857
(Bury St Edmunds, 1911 England census)
*Arthur Shitter was a professor of music; his pupils
must have had a laugh.*

Lottie Shitting
Born Michigan, *c.*1869
(Kalamazoo, Michigan, 1894 Michigan state census)

Theresia [*sic*] Shitting
Born Büttstedt, Germany, *c.*1762

Christian Shitty
Born Saxony, *c.*1806 (Brooklyn, New York, 1860 US census)

Colan Shitwell
(Female) Born Ontario, *c.*1858
(Welland, Ontario, 1891 Canada census)

Shit Woman
Born Alberta, *c.*1869 (Alberta, 1901 Canada census)

Goldie Shower
Born Virginia, *c.*1902 (Baltimore, Maryland, 1920 US census)

Margaret Skidmark
Daughter of Henry Skidmark and Catherine Muldoon;
born St Mary, Jersey City, New Jersey, USA, 29 July 1893;
baptized 3 August 1893

Arson Skidmore
Married Gloucester, 1849

Joseph Slash
Married Lambeth, London, 1858

Fannie Slime
Born Virginia, *c.*1900 (Mecklenburg, Virginia, 1910 US census)

Wash Slime
Born South Carolina, *c.*1844
(Cooper, South Carolina, 1880 US census)

Sarah Splasher
Born Leicester, *c.*1791 (St Luke, Middlesex, 1861 England census)

Brown Spray
Born Thorne, Yorkshire, 1874

Ruby May Spray
Resident of Macquarie, New South Wales, 1930
(1901–36 Australian electoral rolls)

Trannie Sprinkle
(Female) Born South Carolina, USA, 8 August 1895;
died Cowpens, South Carolina, USA, June 1980

Dick Sprinkles
Born Castle Thorpe, Buckinghamshire, *c.*1804
(Castle Thorpe, 1871 England census)

Ashford Squirts
(Male) Born Wellow, Nottinghamshire, *c.*1851
(Greasley, Nottinghamshire, 1871 England census)

Shitty Strange
Born Haselbury, Dorset, *c.*1844 (Haselbury, 1851 England census)

Latrine Topping
Born Warrington, Lancashire, *c.*1871
(Warrington, 1881 England census)

Dick Trickle
Born Lancashire, *c.*1781
(Prescot, Lancashire, 1841 England census)
His son was also called Dick Trickle.

P. Upward
Baptized Stourpaine, Dorset, 25 December 1867

Jesus Urine
Married Reyes Ajala, Santa Cruz, Rosales, Mexico, 1894

Willie Urine
Born California, *c.*1909 (Glendale, Arizona, 1920 US census)

Walks In Shit
(Female) Born *c.*1825 (Dakota Territory, 1886 US Indian census)

Shitty Walsh
(Female) Born Leeds, Yorkshire, *c.*1893
(Leeds, 1911 England census)

Fanny Weed
Married Kettering, Northamptonshire, 1904

Fanny Wetnight
Born Maryland, *c.*1855 (Middleton, Maryland, 1870 US census)

Lulu P. Wetnight
Born Maryland, *c.*1870 (Middletown, Frederick, Maryland,
1880 US census)

SPOONERISMS AND REVERSE NAMES

Funny names, like many jokes, depend on how you say them. With these, you have to say them in reverse, in the style of Smith, John, or transpose their opening letters as a spoonerism. I am sure you will manage to work them out.

Vagina Best
Born c.1926 (Lincoln, Louisiana, 1930 US census)

Joe Blob
Born Wisconsin, c.1896 (Menasha, Wisconsin, 1930 US census)

William Job Blow
Born Lincoln, 1887

Job Blower
Born Stockton, Shropshire, 27 August 1727

Fanny Bushy
Born Middlesex, c.1812 (Whitechapel, London, 1841 census)
She also had a daughter with the same name, born c.1833.

Fanny Cucker
Born Sutton, Surrey, c.1857 (Sutton, 1871 England census)

Pat Fenis
Born c.1875; passenger on *Celtic*, New York, USA–Liverpool, England, arrived 2 August 1913

Kate Grunt
Born Kansas, c.1879 (Homewood, Kansas, 1910 US census)

Mary Hinge
Born Clutton, Somerset, 1846

Cairy Hunt
Born Kentucky, 1884 (Nicholas, Kentucky, 1900 US census)

Fanny Lovely
Baptized Moulton, Lincolnshire, 10 October 1830

Pussy Major
Born Georgia, *c.*1845
(Brownville and Whittens, Lee, Alabama, 1880 US census)

Phyllis [*sic*] Sipp
Born Nebraska, *c.*1915 (Gordon, Nebraska, 1920 US census)
Miss Sipp's name is unremarkable until she has to write it
surname first, whereupon it turns into Sipp, Phyllis.

Pussy Small
Born South Carolina, *c.*1830
(Beaufort, South Carolina, 1870 US census)

Betty Swall
Married Auckland, Durham, 1860

Fanny Tight
Born Ware, Hertfordshire, 1857

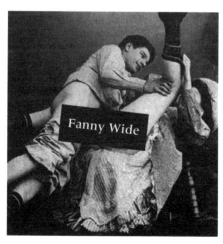

Married Cardiff, Glamorgan, Wales, 1900

OFF THE RECORD

In the United States, the land of the free and the home of the brave – especially when it comes to bizarre names – freedom of information means that no one can hide: online access to US public records, phone books and the like present a diverse range of data about US residents. They are generally thoroughly reliable and record precise addresses and other details, but some of the double entendre names encountered among them are so improbable that they may be imaginative hoaxes or instances of exhibitionists who have deliberately changed their names to attract attention. Outside the examples cited below, there are, for instance, numerous American citizens apparently called Darth Vader, Amanda Hugenkiss and Rip Meoff, and there is apparently a Somebody Anybody and a C. Overleaf. Some names have clearly been inspired by films: Alotta Fagina, as noted on page 63; Ivana Humpalot is the role played by Kristen Johnston in *Austin Powers: The Spy Who Shagged Me* (1999) and Gaylord Focker is the character played by Ben Stiller in *Meet the Parents* (2000) and *Meet the Fockers* (2004). One may speculate on how someone called Suckmy Dick (who appears to live in Old Hardin Road), Randy Midgett (a resident of Stumpy Point) and the dozens of Randy Dykes operate in daily life. I'd be delighted to hear from any of them – if only to see their signatures.

Randy Allday

Duke Asshole

Fabio Assman

Star Balls

Iva Biggun

Windy Bottoms

Gay Bum

Suk Bum

Chastity R. Bumgardner

Bevis Butthead

Chancre Casanova

Janet Cuntlip

Bumboy Curry

Wayne Curz

Suckmy Dick

Woody Dick

Bigg Gus Dickus

Dill Doe

Butch Dyke

Alotta Fagina

Howie Feltersnatch

Willie FisTerboTTom

Patsy Fluffer

Gaylord Focker

Maria Fuckmonkey

Bob Fuckmyself

Randy Git

Dick Gozinya

Ivana Humpalot

Betty Humpter

Buster Hymen

May Icome

Dick Insider

Haywood Jablome

Hugh Jardon

Hugh Jass

Hugh Jorgan

Dick Kuntz

Rusty Kuntz

Phil Latio

Lesbian Lesbia

Connie Lingus

Vulva P. Lipps

Barry McCockiner

Jack Meoff

Randy Midgett

Craven Morehead

Givey Morehead

Eata Mydick

Dixie Normous

Mike Oxbig

Mike Oxlong

Stu Pidfuc

Buggeroff Pissoff

Hugh G. Rection

Jack Schitt

Randy Schmuck

F. E. Seese

Chlamydia Shank

Eric Shon

Nova Gina Sierra

Doggie Styles

Jenna Talia

Venereal Thompson

Thougrod R. Titiporn

Anita Uranus

Crotch Vomit

Pure Vomit

William Whorehouse

Fuk You

ON THE SHELF

Although less true in the age of the Internet, it was once possible for those afflicted with an odd name to be fairly anonymous. Although many writers of fiction seek the cover of a pseudonym, this is not the case with most authors who, with every new work they pen, present the world with their name, often in large type to be prominently displayed in a bookcase. Works by the following authors may be found in bookshops and libraries; one assumes they were the names with which they were born, rather than deliberate coinages, but you never know.

Pierre Anus

Ernst Franz Gustav Assman

Nellie Badcock

Ludwig von Baldass

R. C. Balls

Paula Balls-Organista

Melville Balsillie

Rebecca Hammering Bang

Gay Esty Bangs

Lelia McAnally Batte

Robert Pierce Beaver

Harry Beevers

Krista Bendová

John Thomas Bigge

Johanna Blows

Léon Bollock

Margot Bollock

Hugo Bonk

Frances Bonker

Twat Booth

Nancy Boy

Reynaldo Kuntz Busch

Harry Cock

Ivan Cunt

Hugh Dick

Arsen Diklić

Ben Dover

A. Farto

Semen Frug

Mingyi Fucha

Johann Fück

Stanka Fuckar

Gertrud Fucker

Diego Fucks

Brigitte Fux

Bess Goodykoontz

Hugo Horny

Henry Hornyold-Strickland

Kurt Kink

Joseph Kinky

Bent Koch

Erno Kunt

Arnold Hilarius Kuntz

Harry Kuntz

Dirk La Cock

Bruno Lesbo

Barbara Lube

Benjamin Minge

Miriam Minger

John Muckarsie

Jacques Off

Violet Organ

Giacomo Orifice

Jean Claude Pecker

Else Pée

Emmanuel Perve

William Piddle

Ismo Porn

Willy Prick

Mme J. J. Fouqueau de Pussy

Doris Pogue Screws

Peter M. Semen

Abraham Shag

Theodore Shite

I. I. Shitts

Wolfgang Sucker

André Tosser

E. G. Vagina

Rolf Wank

Ferdinand Germinian Wanker

William Wanker

Just occasionally, a kind of literary determinism comes into play, and authors with unusual names choose – or fate chooses for them – to write on subjects that are either curiously appropriate, or which at least sound to readers with a keen ear for innuendo as though they might be appropriate given the author's name.

Claude Balls, *Shy Men, Sex, and Castrating Women*
San Francisco: Polemic Press, 1985

Mrs M. A. Banger, *Lead the Way Ladies!*
Brighton: Brighton Herald, 1906

Marston Bates, *Gluttons and Libertines: Human Problems of Being Natural*
New York: Random House, 1971

Harry Bone (and Grace Loucks Elliot),
The Sex Life of Youth
New York: Council of Christian Associations, 1929

Anton Bum, *Handbuch der Massage*
Berlin: Urban & Schwarzenberg, 1907

Nonce Casanova, *La Libertine*
Amiens: E. Malfère, 1921

Douglas J. Cock, *Every Other Inch a Methodist*
London, Epworth, 1987

William Cockburn, *The Symptoms, Nature, Cause, and Cure of a Gonorrhoea*
London: G. Strahan, 1713

Nicholas Cox (preface by E. D. Cuming),
The Gentleman's Recreation
London, Cresset Press, 1928

Gordon David Crapper,
Some Examples of Wave Motion in Fluids
Liverpool: Liverpool University Press, 1975

Mari Anus Cuming, *The Drummer Boy*
Detroit: The Author, 1868

Ram Dass, *Miracle of Love*
New York: Dutton, 1979

Eric Fuchs, *Sexual Desire and Love*
Cambridge: James Clarke, 1983

Anita Hardon, et al, *Monitoring Family Planning
and Reproductive Rights*
London: Zed, 1997

Karen Horney, *The Adolescent Diaries
of Karen Horney*
New York: Basic Books, 1980

Benedict Lust, *The Fountain of Youth*
New York: Macfadden Publications, 1923

Helmut Puff, *Sodomy in Reformation Germany
in Switzerland, 1400–1600*
Chicago: University of Chicago Press, 2003

Robert H. Rimmer, *The X-Rated Videotape Guide*
New York: Arlington House, 1984

Timothy Sex, *Coastwise Cruising*
Lymington: Nautical Publishing Co., 1970

Désiré Tits, *La Formation de la Jeunesse*
Brussels: Office de Publicité, 1945

Jacques Tits, *Buildings of Spherical Type
and Finite BN-Pairs*
Berlin: Springer Verlag, 1974

PERFECT PAIRS

There is said to be a divinity that shapes our ends, but there is clearly also some power that leads people with certain names to marry. In some instances this may be to the bride's advantage, trading in an unfortunate name for a more acceptable one. Good was clearly an improvement on Fucker, whereas swapping Good for Tosser was a move in the wrong direction, just as Penis was a poor exchange for Saucy. Or it can be a no-win situation, as when Marie Angèle Le Coq married François August Anus in Paris on 19 June 1892, and went from being a Coq to an Anus. To compound the issue, the American way of using one's maiden name along with one's new surname is a minefield – unless Ella Fister was thereafter happy to be known as Mrs Fister–McAnally. Sadly, there are a number of 'ones that got away' – pairings that appear to be genuine, but lack corroboration, among them the marriages that joined Beaver–Wetter, Busch–Graber, Busch–Rash, Cox–Ucker, Filler–Quick, Kuntz–Dick, Long–Wiwi and Rump–Orefice.

Balls–Bottoms

Sandra Balls married Martyn Bottoms, England, 1997

Balls–Hiscock

Clarissa Balls married George Hiscock, St Martin-in-the-Fields, London, 30 June 1818

Ballwell–Daily

Peter Ballwell married Cora Daily, Idaho, USA, 6 May 1908

Beaver–Bush

James Beaver married Winifred H. Bush, West Ham, London, 1921

Best–Lay

Ann Elizabeth Best married Thomas Lay, Montgomery, Illinois, USA, 23 August 1849

Bollock–Nitz
Hannah Bollock married Frank A. Nitz, Grant, South Dakota,
USA, 22 September 1933

Bottom–Butt
Harold Bottom married May Butt, England, 1989

Brown–Beaver
Nathanial [*sic*] Brown married Sophia Lovetta Beaver, Rowan,
North Carolina, USA, 20 November 1873

Brown–Nipple
Margarette Brown married John Nipple, Carroll, Indiana,
USA, 18 March 1876

Bum–Rimer
Orville P. Bum married Bessie Rimer, Hillsboro, Missouri,
USA, 19 May 1926

Bush–Shaver
Jane Eva Bush married Hiram Shaver, Dundas, Ontario,
Canada, 24 August 1880

Butt–Payne
Bernard F. Butt married Elizabeth S. Payne, Wandsworth,
London, 1915

Butts–McAnally
Frank Levi Butts married Bertie McAnally, Harrisonville,
Missouri, USA, 30 December 1908

Butts–McCracken
Crystal Butts married Levi McCracken, USA, 2000

Casanova–Screws
Ricky Casanova married Ginger Screws, USA, 1974

Cock–Balls
Mr B. A. Cock married Mrs M. A. Balls, St Clair, Missouri,
USA, 14 May 1891

Cock–Holder
S. D. Cock married Ellen Holder, Warren, Tennessee,
USA, 25 January 1903

Cocks–Suckling

Florence Cocks married Frederick Suckling, Hunslet, Yorkshire, 1919

Comeson–Dykes

Marie Comeson married William D. Dykes, Cocke, Tennessee, USA, 1 March 1955

Cox–Balls

Tracey Cox married Alison Balls, England, 1989

Cox–Swinger

Emily Cox married Frederick E. Swinger, Islington, London, 1912

Coy–Nude

Robert Coy married Rose Mary Nude, Cook County, Illinois, USA, 22 September 1943

Dick–Ball
Garry Dick married Karina Ball, England, 1988

Dick–Daily
Margaret Dick married William Daily, Randolph, Illinois, USA, 4 April 1854

Dick–Facey
Mary Dick married Frederick Facey, York, Ontario, Canada, 22 September 1915

Dick–Head
William R. Dick Jr married Ruth V. Head, St Louis, Missouri, USA, 2 October 1946

Dick–Holder
Lynette Dick married Martin Holder, England, 1997

Dick–Spray
Nigel Dick married Donna Spray, England, 1989

Everhard–Withall
Joshua Everhard married Elizabeth Withall, St Ann Blackfriars, London, 1822

Fillerup–Standing
Benjamin Fillerup married Karen Standing, USA, 2007

Fillinger–Goode
Michele R. Fillinger married Clayton M. Goode, Fayette, Kentucky, USA, 21 June 1997

Fister–McAnally
Ella M. Fister married Charles D. McAnally, Clarence, Shelby, Missouri, USA, 20 July 1897

Free–Semen
Margaret Free married Herman Semen, Manhattan, New York, USA, 1872

French–Kiss
Billy Lee French married Carol Ann Kiss, Zephyr Cove, Nevada, USA, 29 July 1978

Fuck–Knowls
John A. J. Fuck married Nancy Knowls, Warren County, Indiana, USA, 2 November 1875

Fuck–Koch
Elizabeth Fuck married John L. Koch, Allen County, Indiana, USA, 8 June 1854

Fuck–Wright
James Fuck married Annie Wright, Grey, Ontario, Canada, 3 November 1880

Fucker–Good
Henriette Fucker married Floyd A. Des Good, Golden City, Barton, Missouri, USA, 27 November 1898

Fucks–Allott
George Fucks married Alice Allott, Thurmaston, Leicestershire, 7 May 1764

Fucks–Boner
Henry Fucks married Merand C. Boner, Bethel, Shelby, Missouri, USA, 31 October 1886

Gay–Bottoms

Joseph Luther Gay married Mary Lee Bottoms, Northampton,
North Carolina, USA, 27 December 1952

Gay–Day

Henry Gay married Ada M. Day, Ely, Cambridgeshire, 1912

Good–Head

Rachel Good married George Head, Old Church, St Pancras,
London, 8 June 1794

Good–Lay

Nathan E. Good married Lynda J. Lay, Johnson, Texas, USA,
5 October 1975

Good–Nicewanger
John Good married Mary Nicewanger, Rockingham, Virginia, USA, 22 January 1805

Hard–Cocks
Keith Hard married Jennifer Cocks, England, 1989

Hard–Cox
William D. Hard married Vernelle Cox, Nodaway, Missouri, USA, 26 June 1949

Hard–Stiff
Steven Hard married Teresa Stiff, England, 2003

Harder–Dick
Martin Harder married Mary Dick, USA, 1965

Hardin–Minge
Ida Hardin married Robert Minge, Dale, Alabama, USA, 7 November 1900

Hardy–Cock
Mamie Hardy married Robert H. Cock, Miami, Indiana, USA, 20 March 1894

Harlot–Blows
Thomas Harlot married Elizabeth Blows, Kingston, Cambridgeshire, 3 November 1809

Hiscock–Shaver
Eliza Hiscock married Burras Shaver, Middlesex, Ontario, Canada, 29 December 1909

Hiscockes–Long
John Hiscockes married Dusabella Long, Warminster, Wiltshire, 24 October 1710

Horney–Horny
Lydia Horney married Jonathan Horny, Guilford, North Carolina, USA, 18 February 1824

Horny–Person
Michel Horny married Marie Alines Person, Paris, France, 3 January 1886

Huge–Bender

Bertha C. Huge married John F. Bender, Adams County, Indiana,
USA, 1 October 1896

Kissee–Dick

Bettie Kissee married William A. Dick, Pulaski, Kentucky,
USA, 20 February 1896

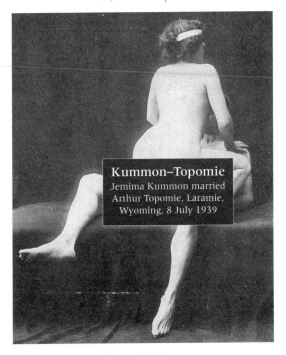

Kummon–Topomie
Jemima Kummon married
Arthur Topomie, Laramie,
Wyoming, 8 July 1939

Kunt–Driver

Harun Kunt married Susan Driver, Wales, 1997

Large–Butt

Lottie L. Large married Francis H. Butt, Cirencester,
Gloucestershire, 1913

Large–Cox

Dinah Large married Thomas Cox, Southrop, Gloucestershire,
10 February 1835

Lick–Ball

Jona Lick married Rachell Ball, McDonald, Missouri, USA,
16 March 1899

Little–Cock

Maud Little married William J. Cock, St Columb, Cornwall, 1925

Little–Cuntesse

Martha Little married Thomas Cuntesse, Ryme Intrinsica,
Dorset, 2 April 1638

Long–Cocks

Emily Long married Frederick Cocks, Nottingham, 1915

Long–Dick

Lizzie D. Long married J. C. Dick, Jefferson, Kentucky, USA,
18 May 1906

Long–Organ

Ada Long married John Organ, Doncaster, Yorkshire, 1916

Love–Hiscock

Thomas W. Love married Annie A. Hiscock, Axminster,
Devon, 1914

Manhood–Cumings

May C. Manhood married Edward C. Cumings, West Ham,
Essex, 1926

Moaney–Virgin

Mary Moaney married James H. Virgin, Bollinger, Missouri,
USA, 7 February 1880

Morecock–Beaver

John Morecock Jr married Marcella Beaver, USA, 1977

Mycock–Rose

Clara V. Mycock married Walter Rose, Wallsall,
Staffordshire, 1925

Pain–Arsley

Robert Pain married Eleanor Arsley, Codsall, Staffordshire,
2 August 1778

Prick–Skinner

William Prick married Ann Skinner, Bury St Edmunds, Suffolk,
25 January 1793

Queer–Dickover

Joseph H. Queer married Susan Dickover, Hamilton, Indiana,
USA, 6 September 1861

Quick–Lay

Paul Quick married Sara Lay, England, 1989

Rampant–Amour

Louis-René Rampant married Marie-Eugenie Amour,
La Celle-sous-Chantemerle, France, 14 July 1790

Riske–Fucks

Henry F. Riske married Maria Elisa Fucks, St Charles, Missouri,
USA, 13 October 1857

Rogers–Bottoms

Thomas Rogers married Winifred Bottoms, England, 1993

Rogers–Daily

Willie Rogers married Marie Daily, Hamblen, Tennessee,
USA, 2 February 1927

Rogers–Hiscock

Broom Rogers married Mary Hiscock, Calne, Wiltshire, 21 May 1809

Rogers–Mewell

W. J. Rogers married Mary F. Mewell, Giles, Tennessee, USA,
23 May 1884

Saucy–Penis

Francoise Saucy married Jean Nicolas Penis, Saint-Mard,
Luxembourg, 19 May 1805

Scorching–Studd

Rebecca Scorching married James Studd, St Leonard's, Shoreditch,
London 14 October 1818

Semen–Bowls
F. M. Semen married Amanda J. Bowls, Iron, Missouri, USA,
3 March 1878

Sex–Hunt
Anna Sex married Thomas Hunt, Chalfont St Peter,
Buckinghamshire, 16 October 1586

Sex–Sore
Mary Sex married Robert Sore, Derby, England, 24 November 1666

Seymour–Bottom
William J. Seymour married Jane E. Bottom, Wandsworth,
London, 1912

Seymour–Bush
William J. Seymour married Rose Bush, West Ham, Essex, 1919

Seymour–Butts
J. P. Seymour married Jennie Butts, Randolph, Missouri, USA,
21 June 1916

Seymour–Cocks
Louisa Seymour married George H. Cocks, Thame,
Oxfordshire, 1926

Seymour–Dick
Matthew Seymour married Beverley Dick, England, 1995

Sharp–Hardcock
Alpha Jane Sharp married Charles C. Hardcock, Carroll County,
Missouri, USA, 19 November 1848

Shave–Bush
Mary Shave married George Bush, Yetminster, Dorset,
20 August 1787

Shmuck–Wood
Eliza Shmuck married Zachariah Wood, Grant, Indiana, USA,
30 December 1882

Slack–Bottom
Fanny Slack married Frederick Charles Bottom, Belper,
Derbyshire, 1878

Slutty–Ball
Abner Slutty married S. Jennie Ball, Ashland, Ohio, USA,
14 May 1863

Spunk–Rizer
Gail B. Spunk married Lena B. Rizer, Levenworth, Kansas, 15 April
1907

Stiff–Cox
Perenel A. Stiff married Charles L. Cox, East Staffordshire, 1987

Street–Walker
Florence Street married Frederick Walker, Wolverhampton,
Staffordshire, 1913

Sukan–Dick
Aganetha Sukan married Abraham B. Dick, Aberdeen, Idaho,
USA, 3 June 1917

Swallows–Cox
Rosemary Swallows married George Cox, USA, 1983

Swift–Cock
Hannah A. Swift married Henry Cock, Delaware, Indiana, USA,
1 April 1860

Swift–Dick
Sarah Swift married Arthur Dick, Hull, Yorkshire, 1924

Tosser–Good
Peter Tosser married Clara Good, Vermillion, Indiana, USA,
21 August 1892

Turner–Over

George H. Turner married Winnifred [*sic*] Over, Greenwich,
London, 1916

Wacker–Dickoff

Herbert Wacker married Catherine Dickoff, Cook County, Illinois,
USA, 20 November 1935

Wang–Holder

Xiaomei Wang married Dick Holder, England, 1998

Wang–King

Yuan Wang married John King, England, 1997

Wanker–Klaus

Henry C. Wanker married Louisa Klaus, Vigo, Indiana,
USA, 16 May 1901

*To those with vivid imaginations, this unfortunate pairing appears
to offer corroboration that Santa Claus comes down the chimney.*

Weedon–Hiscock

Charles Weedon married Amelia Hiscock, Ickenham, Middlesex,
15 December 1830

Wood–Donger

Cecily M. Wood married Reginald R. Donger, Shifnal,
Staffordshire, 1914

Woolly–Shag

Isabel Woolly married Aaron Shag, Tazewell, Illinois, USA,
1 August 1858

Young–Gaylove

Eliza Young married William Gaylove, Clerkenwell, London, 1817

Young–Slapper

Laura Young married William Slapper, Henry, Missouri, USA,
31 August 1884

CHAPTER 3

OWN GOAL?

Here follows a gallery of sportspersons whose prowess is matched only by their heroism in placing themselves before the public with such names, frequently even emblazoning them on their shirts. Often they are completely innocuous names in their own countries, but such is the international nature of modern sport that many find themselves playing in countries where their names raise a smile, or more. This was particularly the case during a match in the 2007 Thai Open tennis tournament between Wang Yeu-Tzuoo (Taiwan) and Phillip King (USA), when commentators vainly struggled to avoid referring to the Wang–King game.

Chiqui Arce
Born 1972; Paraguayan; footballer
His real name is Francisco – he celebrated his nickname by displaying it on his shirt.

Andrei Arshavin
Born 1981; Russian; footballer

Ars Bandeet
Algerian; footballer

Segar Bastard
Born 1854; died 1921; English; footballer
*Became a referee and was in charge of
the 1879 FA Cup final and the first ever
England vs Wales match in 1879 –
thereby confirming most spectators' view
that all referees are bastards.*

Chief Bender
Born 1884; died 1954; American;
baseball player
*His full name was Charles Albert
Bender. He was a member of the Ojibwa
tribe, hence being known as 'Chief'.*

Phil Boggs
Born 1949; died 1990; Canadian; diver

Radek Bonk
Born 1976; Czechoslovakian; ice hockey player

Lee Bum-Ho
Born 1981; South Korean; baseball player

Dick Burns
Born 1863; died 1937; American; baseball player

Homer Bush
Born 1972; American; baseball player

Randy Bush
Born 1958; American; baseball player

Dick Butkus
Born 1942; American; American footballer

Grant Clitsome
Born 1985; Canadian; ice hockey player

Harry Colon
Born 1969; American; American footballer

Chubby Cox
Born 1955; American; basketball player
Born John Arthur Cox III.

Lorraine Crapp
Born 1938; Australian; swimmer

Luca Cunti
Born 1989; Swiss; ice hockey player

Dick Curl
Born 1940; American; American footballer

Harry Dick
Born 1920; died 2002; Canadian; ice hockey player

Paul Dickov
Born 1972; Scottish; footballer

'Ugly' Johnny Dickshot
Born 1910; died 1997; American; baseball player

De'Cody Fagg
Born 1984; American; American footballer

Rod Fanni
Born 1981; French; footballer

Uwe Fuchs
Born 1966; German; footballer

Gregor Fucka
Born 1971; Slovenian; basketball player

Argelico 'Argel' Fucks
Born 1974; Brazilian; footballer
His name has given rise to such headlines as, in 2001,
Eurosport.com's 'Fucks off to Benfica'.

Milan Fukal
Born 1975; Czechoslovakian; footballer

Kosuke Fukudome
Born 1977; Japanese; baseball player

Yutaka Fukufuji
Born 1982; Japanese; ice hockey player

B. J. Gaylord
Canadian; ice hockey player

CAPT. JACK GLASSCOCK.
ALLEN & GINTER'S
RICHMOND, Cigarettes. VIRGINIA.

Jack Glasscock
Born 1857; died 1947; American; baseball player

Jimmy Gobble
Born 1981; American; baseball player

David Goodwillie
Born 1989; Scottish; footballer

Bernt Haas
Born 1978; Austrian; footballer

Fair Hooker
Born 1947; American; American footballer

Mike Hunt
Born 1956; American; American footballer

Misty Hyman
Born 1979; American; swimmer

Andreas Ivanschitz
Born 1983; Austrian; footballer

Aase Schiøtt Jacobsen
Danish; badminton player

Rusty Kuntz
Born 1955; American; baseball player

Stefan Kuntz
Born 1962; German; footballer

Pete LaCock
Born 1952; American; baseball player

Ivana Mandic
Born 1979; Serbian; basketball player
She is known as 'Ivi'.

Luke Myring
Born 1983; English; Rugby Union player

Dick Passwater
Born 1921; American; NASCAR driver

Corey Pecker
Born 1981; Canadian; ice hockey player

Gaylord Perry
Born 1938; American; baseball player

Brian Pinas
Born 1978; Dutch; footballer

Dick Pole
Born 1950; American; baseball player

Lucious Pusey
Born 1984; American; American football player
He legally changed his name to Lucious Seymour.

Quim
Born 1975; Portuguese; footballer
The goalkeeper's full name is Joaquim Manuel Sampaio da Silva,
but he plays under his nickname, Quim.

Alf Sandercock
Australian; lawn bowls player

Rafael Scheidt
Born 1976; Brazilian; footballer

Dick Seaman
Born 1913; died 1939; English;
Grand Prix driver

Anatoli Semenov
Born 1962; Russian; ice hockey player

Dick Shiner
Born 1942; American;
American footballer

Danny Shittu
Born 1980; Nigerian; footballer

Assol Slivets
Born 1982; Belarusian; skier

Craphonso Thorpe
Born 1983; American;
American footballer

Lyudmila Titova
Born 1946; Russian; speed skater

Dick Trickle
Born 1941; American; race car driver

Ron Tugnutt
Born 1967; Canadian; ice hockey player

Roberto López Ufarte
Born 1958; Spanish; footballer

Semen Varlamov
Born 1988; Russian; ice hockey player
His birth name – Simeon Aleksandrovich Varlamov – was anglicized to 'Semen Varlamov' when listed by the Washington Capitals (2006).

Andreas Wank
Born 1988; German; ski-jumper

Dick Wantz
Born 1940; died 1965; American; baseball player

Mike Weir
Born 1970; Canadian; golfer
His name is sometimes unkindly mispronounced as 'My Queer'.

Dean Windass
Born 1969; English; footballer

WHAT A PERFORMANCE

FILM CREDITS

Names that appear in film credits must be treated with some circumspection. Many actors and actresses change their names from birth names that may have had embarrassing connotations, others have carried on regardless, while, in the realm of pornography, the necessity to contrive ever-more graphic names, from Candy Cantaloupes to Long Dong Silver, has resulted in some gems. Of course, such names break the rules in that they were deliberately contrived, rather than being 'real' names and accidental double entendres – or were they? Could there perhaps be some sort of nominative determinism at work here, where a person's name leads him or her into an appropriate profession? After all, if your name happens to be Felicity Fellatio, a job in primary education is probably not going to happen.

REAL* NAMES (OR, THE ACTRESS FORMERLY KNOWN AS FLUCK...)

Jeremy Anus
Actor; *Car Jack* (2008)

Allys Arsel
Actress; *The Haunted Castle* (1923)

Heidi Bollock
Editor, director; *River Right of Passage* (2008)

Kum Young Bum
Animator; *Fullmetal Alchemist 2: Curse of the Crimson Elixir* (2004 video game)

Maiana Bum
Actress; *O Cometa* (Brazilian TV mini-series, 1989)

* As far as can be established.

Zvi Bums
Musician; *Hebrew Song & Chorus Festival* (1978 TV movie)

Doris Condom
Actress; *Any Given Sunday* (1999)

Edwige Cunati
Born 1907; died 1998; actress
This French film actress's name changed to Edwige Feuillère
upon her marriage.

Ima Cunt
Director; *Wonders of the Unseen World* (1927)

Diana Fluck
Born 1931; died 1984; actress

The original name of British actress Diana Dors. 'They asked me to change my name', because, she explained, 'I suppose they were afraid that if my real name, Diana Fluck, was in lights, and one of the lights blew...' As she related in her autobiography, she was once asked to open a fête in her home town of Swindon. During lunch with the local vicar she revealed her real name. That afternoon, the vicar, worried at pronouncing 'Fluck' correctly, introduced her to the crowd with, 'Ladies and gentlemen, it is with great pleasure that I introduce to you our star guest. We all love her, especially as she is our local girl. I therefore feel it right to introduce her by her real name; ladies and gentlemen, please welcome the very lovely Miss Diana Clunt.'

Lars Fuck
Composer; *Who's the Greatest* (2003)

Isaac Fucks
Director; *O Esôfago da Mesopotâmia* (Brazil, 1998)

Sarah Jane Fulks
Born 1917; died 2007; actress

The real name of Jane Wyman, first wife of Ronald Reagan.

Pamela Jayne Hardon
Born 1950; actress; *Carrie* (1976), *Halloween* (1978)

The birth name of P. J. Soles , the German-born actress, formerly married to Dennis Quaid.

Lois Ruth Hooker
Born 1927; died 2007; actress

The original name of Canadian actress Lois Maxwell who played Miss Moneypenny in fourteen James Bond films.

Harmon Killacunt
Actor; *Dear Pam* (1976)

Maria Labia
Born 1880; died 1955; actress; *Il Re d'Inghilterra non paga* (1941)

Joanne Letitia LaCock

Born 1922; died 1996; actress

The real name of US film star Joanne Dru.

Ewa Minge

Born 1968

A Polish fashion designer, she appeared as herself in the Polish TV comedy series Niania: Pokaz mody *(2007).*

Lynnea Minger

Actress; *Joey* (1985)

Drew Peacock

Stuntman; *Carpool* (1996)

Jennifer Shag

Actress; *Automatons* (2006)

Jean Shufflebottom

Born 1928; actress

The real name of British actress Jeanie Carson.

Claire Tits

Actress; *Met voorbedachten rade: Wurgmoord in M.P.I.*
(1982 Belgian TV mini-series)

Olga Vagina

Sound department; *Tantsy na kryshe* (1985 USSR movie)

Jordan M. Wank

Executive producer; *Devil Times Five* (1974)

Thomas Wanker

Composer; *The Day After Tomorrow* (2004)

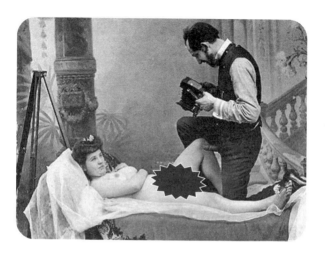

BLUE MOVIE MONIKERS

Alyssa Alps
Mountainous Mams (1993)

Ben Asslick
The Sum of All Rears (2002)

Boroka Balls
Private Tropical 29: Sluts and Coconuts (2006),
Teenage Jizz Junkies 3 (2006)

Swiss Balls
Aka Eric Swiss; *Wet Food 2* (2007), *Big Sloppy Asses* (2008)

Cunty Ballz
The Mind (2009)

Choklat Beaver
Mz. Mildred Bulge (1998)

Betty Boobs
Bra Breakers Vol. 1 (1988)

Sasha Brabuster
Tittylicious (2005)

Bumfuck
Little White Chicks and Big Black Monster Dicks 13 (2001)

Candy Cantaloupes
Boobarella (1992), *Bosom Buddies* (2002)

Prick Cavett
Sex Stalker (1983)

Clarissa Climax
Blowjob Adventures of Dr Fellatio 19 (1999)

Loretta Clitora
Blowjob Adventures of Dr Fellatio 33 (2001)

Anita Cock
MILF School 4 (2007)

Carole Comes
Aka Carole Miller; *Granny's Gang Bang 3 (1999), Pussy Fingers 5 (2002)*

Liq Cum
Black Swallowers 1 (2000)

Tony Cumallova
Smartass (2004)

Catalina Cumalot
Chunky Mature Women 3 (2004)

Cathy Cumshot
Pig Fuckers 2 (2003)

Cumswalla
Aka Cumswalla Candy; *In the Thick 7 (2003)*

Cali Cumz
Ass Factor 4 (2006)

Nicole Cunt
Inner City Black Cheerleader Search 63 (2004)

Treasure Cunt
Monster Booty 5 (2007), To Pee or Not to Pee (2007)

Toppsy Curvey
Score Busty Covergirls Vol. 1: Busty Dusty & Toppsy Curvey (1994)

Strechy Dick
Freaks of Nature: The Next Generation (2003)

Too Long Dong
Selena Under Siege (1995)

Busty Dusty
Boob Cruise Babes Vol. 3 (1999)

Erik Everhard
Dick Sucking Anal Bitches of Fresh Meat (2007)

Felicity Fellatio
Awakening (role: Busty Gypsy Zombie) (2006)

Jayme Fuckingham
Tea Baggers 3 (2003)

Johnny Fucknose
Excuse Me…Volume 23 (2004)

Lance Goodthrust
Thunderballs (1998)

Dave Hardman
Cum Swapping Sluts 7 (2004)

Rock Hardon
Widespread (1995)

Heidi Hooters
Big Boob Girls Around the World 7: Tit to Tit (1991)

Nikki Knockers
Big Boob Girls Around the World 15 (1992)

Little Oral Annie
Hard to Swallow (1985)

Sabrina Love-Cox
Eating Poussé (2002)

Mangina
Freaks of Nature: The Next Generation (2003)

Mastah Meat
Slut Safari (1994)

Mandy Morecock
Inner City Black Cheerleader Search 64 (2004)

Chesty Morgan
Deadly Weapons (1974)

Melissa Mounds
Flesh Gordon Meets the Cosmic Cheerleaders (1989)

Melonee Mounds
Busty Auditions 3 (2001)

Dick Nasty
British Butt Bangers (1998), *Big Boob Butt Bangers 5* (2006)

Kimmie Nipples
XL Girls: Home Alone Volume 2 (2004)

Nick Nude
Swallow My Rod & Share the Wad (2005)

Wilde Oscar
Blowjob Adventures of Dr Fellatio 9 (1998)

Pandora Peaks
Aka Stephanie Schick; *Lesbian Big Boob Bangeroo* (2002)

Dick Rambone
Backdoor Brides (1986)

Randi Ravage
Dirty Bob's Xcellent Adventures 30: Lost in the Cleavage (1997)

Max Schlong
Leather Bears and Smooth Chested Huskies (2005)

Lotta Semen
Meatball (1972)

Flick Shagwell
Lezervoir Dogs (2003)

Long Dong Silver
Beauty and the Beast (1982)

Norma Stitz
Under the Big Tops (1997)

Betty Swallows
Gangsta' Bang 6 (2003)

Johnny Thrust
Big Boob Squirting Nurses (2006)

Traci Topps
Big Boob Mamathon (1996)

Plenty Uptopp
Mega-Boob Olympics (2002)

Booty Von Felcher
Itty Bitty Titty Jail Babes (2001)

Vince Voyeur
Big Load Ahead (2005)

Kelly Fuck'n Wells
Spunk'd 4 (2006)

Wendy Whoppers
Aka Tommy Tatas; *Environmental Attorney* (1993),
Humongous Hooters (1994)

BANNED BANDS?

Provocatively named bands date especially from the punk era, which generated such celebrated examples as the Sex Pistols. Some of these are arguably no sillier than successful bands such as Mott the Hoople, Throbbing Gristle or Hootie & the Blowfish and some may actually have existed long enough to be banned from appearing or publicizing their events – an inherent drawback they perhaps overlooked in devising their names – while others may never have got beyond the perfervid drawing boards of their members.

Even classical musicians are not immune. Many play word games during downtime in rehearsals, one of which is to devise fantasy ensembles – Josef Suk, Yo-Yo Ma and Felix Kok, for example, might get together and form the Suk Ma Kok trio.

4-Skins

Anal Beard Barbers

Anal Sausage

Ancient Chinese Penis

Anus the Menace

Armageddon Dildos

Arse Destroyer

Assück

Barbara's Bush

Barney Rubble and the Cunt Stubble

Beast Penis

Big Daddy Cumbuckets

Bloated Scrotum

Blow Job Queen

Bolt Upright and the Erections

Buster Hymen and the Penetrators

Butt Full of Dick

Butthole Surfers

Celebrity Glass Eye Anal Beads

Cheetah Chrome Motherfuckers

Cocks in Stained Satin

Crazy Penis

Crucifucks

The Cunning Runts

Cunts With Attitude

Defecation

Dick Delicious and the Tasty Testicles

Dogfuckers

Dog Shit Taco

Dripping Horse Cock

Exploding Fuck Dolls

Flaming Fuckheads

Foreskin 500

Fuckhead

The Fucking Cunts

Fuck Me, Suck Me, Call Me Helen

Fuckshitpiss

Fudge Tunnel

FUs

GG Allin and the Scumfucs

Grand Mother Fucker

Hard-Ons

Harry and the Mulefuckers

Harry Pussy

Hugh Jorgan and the Four Skins

Imperial Butt Wizards

Jack Off Jill

Jehovah's Wetness

The Jizzbuckets

Johnny McPenis and the Ass Clams

Killer Pussy

Kitten Felcher

Lubricated Goat

Lubricunts

Man-Sized Action

Mighty Sphincter

Neurotic Arseholes

Penetrators

Penis DeMilo

Penis Flytrap

Penis Genius

Penis Pulling Ramrods of Death

Revolting Cocks

Sarcastic Orgasm

Schlong

Seemen

Señor Cummypants

Sic Fucks

Slits

Smegma

Spermbirds

Split Beaver

Supersuckers

The Throbbing Testicles

Vaginal Davis

Vibrators

Brahms

CHAPTER 5

Liszt

RHYMING SLANG
PEOPLE

The names of real and fictitious people have long been used in cockney rhyming slang – so long, in fact, that several of the examples here refer to historical figures including medieval monarchs, Maria Monk (spunk), an early nineteenth-century Canadian nun who was the subject of a sensational book published in 1836 and General Smuts (nuts), the South African prime minister 1939–48. It is highly dynamic, however, often being updated as suitable candidates emerge from the ranks of celebrities, characters in TV programmes and sportspeople. Such usage tends to be more ephemeral – for which reason (and the laws of libel) they are excluded.

arsehole
Roy Castle, King Cole

balls
Henry Hall(s), Nobby Hall(s), Max Wall(s)

bent
Clark Kent, Duke of Kent

bollocks
Jackson Pollock(s)

bum
Tom Thumb

crap
Andy Capp, Von Trapp

cunt
Anthony Blunt, Ethan Hunt, Gareth Hunt, James Hunt

dyke
Magnus Pyke

fanny
Orphan Annie, Jackie Danny

fart/tart
Lionel Bart, D'Oyly Carte

fuck
Uncle Buck, Donald Duck

fuck it
Charlie Bucket

fuck off
Vincent van Gogh

fucked
Friar Tuck(ed)

go down
Divine Brown

goolies
Tom Doolies (from US folk song character Tom Dooley)

hard (erection)
Marquis de Sade

homo
Perry Como

horn
Marquis of Lorne

knob
Uncle Bob

melons (breasts)
Sue Ellens

nuts (testicles)
General Smuts

pee
Bruce Lee, Gypsy Rose Lee

piddle
Jimmy Riddle, Nelson Riddle

piss
(Sir) Arthur Bliss, Alger Hiss

pissed
Brahms and Liszt, Oliver Twist

ponce
Charlie Ronce

poof
Nelly Duff

poop
Ali Oop

queer
King Lear

shit
Martin Chuzzlewit, William Pitt

shite
Barry White

slash (urinate)
Arthur Ashe, Johnny Cash, Ogden Nash

spunk
Maria Monk

stupid cunt
Cupid Stunt (Kenny Everett character)

titty
Walter Mitty

turd
Thora Hird, Henry the Third, Richard the Third

wank
Ann Frank, J. Arthur Rank

whore
Thomas Moore

DIRTY OLD TOWN:
THE WORLD ATLAS
OF RUDE PLACES

Sadly, political correctness has resulted in the 'cleaning up' of many explicit place names, especially in North America, where Whorehouse Meadow, Oregon, became Naughty Girl Meadow and Nellie's Nipple, Arizona, is now College Peak. Similarly, Brassiere Hills, Alaska, and Squaw Tit are no more – although some have been retained after public campaigns, such as that mounted to keep Dildo, a phallic peninsula jutting into Spread Eagle Bay, Newfoundland.

In England in 2009, Lewes District Council, East Sussex, flew in the face of trivial concerns, such as the state of the economy, in favour of issuing a directive banning street names that might possibly fall foul of double entendre interpretation. The county town of Lewes itself already boasts a Juggs Lane (named for the route followed by the women who once strode across the downs from Brighthelmston – Brighton – with their donkeys laden with panniers, or jugs, of fish) and a Cockshut Road (the name of which refers to the trapping of woodcocks at twilight, 'cock-shut time', as Shakespeare calls it in *Richard III*). Despite their historic associations, such names would no longer pass muster if the council had its way, and neither would Corfe Close. 'Why?' you may ask. Because someone would have to live at No. 4, so their address would be '4 Corfe Close' (it may take several repetitions of the name before you get their drift on that one). If Lewes District Council, and those who share their views, were in charge of town and street naming nationally or internationally, none of the following would have been approved.

UK

Back Passage, London, EC1
Backside Lane, Banbury, Oxfordshire
The Bastard, Argyll and Bute

The Occupier,
Beaver Close,
Morden,
Surrey

Bell End, Hereford and Worcester

Booty Lane, Great Heck, North Yorkshire

Bottoms Fold, Mossley, Greater Manchester

Brown Willy, Cornwall

Bush, Cornwall

Butt Hole Lane, Conisbrough, South Yorkshire

Cocklick End, Lancashire

Cocks, Cornwall

Cockshoot Close, Whitney, Oxfordshire

Cockup, Cumbria

Crotch Crescent, Marston, Oxfordshire

Dicks Mount, Burgh St Peter, Norfolk

Dyke, Lincolnshire

Faggot, Northumberland

Fanny Avenue, Killmarsh, Derbyshire

Fanny Burn, Perth and Kinross

Fanny Hands Lane, Ludford, Lincolnshire

Fingringhoe, Essex

Great Tosson, Northumberland

Gropecunt Lane

Gropecuntelane (c.1230) contains the earliest dated use of 'cunt'
in the Oxford English Dictionary. *It was traditionally the place*
where prostitutes worked, with examples in London (renamed
Grub Street and, since 1830, Milton Street), Oxford (later Grope,
now Grove Lane), Bristol, Newcastle and Dublin.

Happy Bottom, Corfe Mullen, Dorset

Hole of Horcum, North Yorkshire

Hooker Road, Norwich, Norfolk

Lickers Lane, Prescot, Merseyside

Lickey End, Bromsgrove, West Midlands

Lickham Bottom, Devon

Little Bushey Lane, Bushey, Hertfordshire

Long Lover Lane, Halifax, West Yorkshire

Lord Hereford's Knob, Powys

Lower Swell, Stow-on-the-Wold, Gloucestershire

Menlove Avenue, Liverpool, Merseyside

Merkins Avenue, West Dumbarton

Mincing Lane, London, EC3

Minge Lane, Upton-upon-Severn, Worcestershire

Moisty Lane, Marchington, Staffordshire

Muff, Donegal

Nob End, Bolton, Greater Manchester

Nork Rise, Banstead, Surrey

Old Sodom Lane, Dauntsey, Wiltshire

Pant, Oswestry, Shropshire

Penistone, South Yorkshire

Percy Passage, London, W1

Pratts Bottom, Orpington, Kent

Prince Albert Court, Surrey

Pump Alley, Hounslow, Middlesex

Ramsbottom Lane, Bury, Greater Manchester

Rimswell, East Yorkshire

St Mellons, Cardiff

Sandy Balls, Hampshire

Scratchy Bottom, Dorset

Shitterton, Dorset

Slag Lane, Lowton, Cheshire

Snatchup, Redbourn, St Albans, Hertfordshire

Swallow Passage, London, W1

Swell, Fivehead, Somerset

Three Cocks, Powys

Titty Ho, Raunds, Wellingborough,
Northamptonshire

Tosside, Lancashire

Twathats, Dumfries and Galloway

Twatt, Orkney

Upper Dicker, East Sussex

Weedon, Northamptonshire

Wetwang, East Yorkshire

Wham Bottom Lane, Rochdale, Lancashire

Willey, Rugby, Warwickshire

Winkle Street, Southampton, Hampshire

THE AMERICAS

Assawoman, Virginia, USA
*Originally spelled Asswaman, it was changed to its current
spelling in 1966 when the Board on Geographic Names did the
reverse of its usual practice and altered it to something offering
more, rather than less, double entendre potential.*

Bald Knob, Arkansas, USA

Balls Falls, Ontario, Canada

Beaver, Oklahoma, USA

Beaver, Oregon, USA

Beaver City, Utah, USA

Beaver Crossing, Nebraska, USA

Beaver Head, Idaho, USA

Beaver Lick, Kentucky, USA

Big Beaver, Saskatchewan, Canada

Big Beaver Lick, Kentucky, USA

Big Bone Lick State Park, Kentucky, USA

Big Knob, Kentucky, USA

Bloody Dick Swamp, South Carolina, USA

Climax, Colorado, USA

Crotch Lake, Ontario, Canada

Cum, Wanderlandia, Tocantins, Brazil

Cum, Zelaya, Nicaragua

Dick Lick Springs, Arkansas, USA

Dildo, Trinity Bay, Newfoundland, Canada
*After Gayside, Newfoundland changed its name because of its
sexual connotations, a local resident tried to change the name of
his village. His fellow inhabitants rejected his suggestion,
however, preferring to retain the name Dildo.*

Dump, Manchester, Jamaica

Erect, Randolph County, North Carolina, USA

Fanny, West Virginia, USA

Felch, Michigan, USA

Felchville, Massachusetts, USA

Finger, North Carolina, USA

French Lick, Indiana, USA

Fruitdale, South Dakota, USA

Gayville, South Dakota, USA

Gobblers Knob, Pennsylvania, USA
*The home of Punxsutawney Phil, the groundhog featured in the
film* Groundhog Day *(1993) – which was largely filmed in
Woodstock, Illinois.*

Hooker, Oklahoma, USA

HORNEYTOWN

North
Carolina, USA

Intercourse, Pennsylvania, USA

Knob Lick, Missouri, USA

Little Dix Village, Anguilla

Mianus, Connecticut, USA

Minge, Haiti

Pis Pis River, Nicaragua

Probe, Utah, USA

Shaft, Pennsylvania, USA

Shafter, California, USA

Shitagoo Lake, Quebec, Canada

Sugar Tit, South Carolina, USA

Tillicum Beach, Alberta, Canada

Wankers Corner, Clackamas, Oregon, USA

Wanks River, Nicaragua

Wet Beaver Creek, Arizona, USA

Woody, Cumberland, Tennessee, USA

EUROPE

Anus, France

(Cascade d') Arse, France

Arsoli, Italy

Buger, Majorca, Spain

Bum, Qabala, Azerbaijan

Busty Hill, Dublin, Ireland

Clit, Romania

Condom, France

Crap, Albania

Craponne-sur-Arzon, France

Cunt, Spain

Cunter, Switzerland

Effin, Limerick, Ireland

Feces de Abaixo (Lower Feces), Spain

Fist, Albania

Fjuckby, Sweden

Austria

Despite its town signs being repeatedly stolen by English-speaking tourists, the residents of Fucking voted in 2004 not to change its name, instead taking steps to make the signs thief-proof.

Horn, Iceland

Labia, Belgium

Minge, Belgium

Muff, Donegal, Ireland

Nobber, Donegal, Ireland

Nork, Yerevan

Pis, Spain

Poo, Spain

Puke, Albania

Pussy, France

Rimsting, Germany

Semen, Moldova

Slut, Västerbotten, Sweden

Spurt, Belgium

Stiff, France

Tit, Russia

Tos, Germany

Turda, Romania

Vagina, Russia

Wank, Germany

*The Wank website (www.wank-haus.de/webcam.html) provides a
live webcam panoramic view from the Wank Haus, while the
official website formerly offered 'Directions to Wank'.*

ASIA

Anus, Papua, Indonesia

Bollock, Philippines

Bottom, Netherlands Antilles

Cumbum, Andhra Pradesh, India

Cunt, Turkey

Dikshit, India

Dong, Yunan, China

Dong Rack, Thailand/Cambodia border

Fukem, Honshu, Japan

Fuku, Shensi, China

Fukue, Honshu, Japan

Gash, Iran

Kunt, Punjab, Pakistan

Moist, Myanmar

Phuket, Thailand

Poo, Himachal Pradesh, India

Rim, Thailand

Semen, Indonesia

Sexmoan, Philippines

Shag Island, Indian Ocean

Shit, Iran

Tong Fuk, South Lantau, Hong Kong, China

Urin, Papua New Guinea

AUSTRALASIA

Bald Knob, New South Wales

Black Charlie's Opening, Tasmania

Bumbang, Victoria

Chinaman's Knob, Western Australia

Iron Knob, South Australia

Middle Intercourse Island, Australia

Mount Buggery, Victoria

Shag Point, South of Moeraki, South Island, New Zealand

Tittybong, Victoria

AFRICA

Bum, Sierra Leone

Dongo, Democratic Republic of Congo

Fucu, Mozambique

Fukum, Yemen

Gisum, Nigeria

Iwanhed, Egypt

Pee, Liberia

Poke, Uganda

Rim, Chad

Shagg, Sudan

Shit, Ethiopia

Tampon, Reunion

Tit, Algeria

Wankie, Zimbabwe

CHAPTER 7

WORLD WIDE
WEIRD

With more than 100 million websites on the World Wide Web, it becomes increasingly difficult to come up with a name that is unique, original and memorable and, at the same time, unambiguous. The lack of full points or hyphens can make all the difference between a name being read correctly or mispronounced, often, as they say in the best comedy circles, with hilarious consequences. Some may well have been deliberately designed to attract attention, others are purely accidental; the fact that a high proportion of them are either defunct or up for sale suggests they failed to attract the right sort of visitors. There are lessons to be learned here, among them that unless a site is offering specialist medical services, the word 'exchange' in an address should NEVER be preceded by a word ending in 's' and that caution is advised in the use of the word 'therapist'.

www.accesstherapist.com
Therapist links

www.actorsexchange.com
Acting links

www.adamsextract.com
Spice and extract company

www.addtherapist.com
Clinical therapist

www.aim4therapist.com
Defunct

www.alterscrap.com
Defunct

www.analemma.com
Astronomy data
*So-called because the Sun's figure-of-eight path
is called an analemma.*

www.artisanalcheese.com
Online cheese shop

www.ass-team.net
German athletic team sponsorship

www.auctionshit.com
Defunct

www.beatleshits.com
Defunct

www.bendover.com
Benjamin Dover's columns

www.bigalsonline.com
Aquarium supplies store

www.bollywoodsmashits.com

Links to movie-related websites

www.budget.co.ck

Cook Islands car rental company

All Cook Islands' business domains end in 'co.ck', but registrations such as 'mybig.co.ck', 'blow.co.ck' or any other name that may be deemed offensive are refused, so relatively few have slipped through the net.

www.childrenswear.co.uk

Children's clothing company

www.choosespain.com

A holiday company

www.comicsexchange.com

Defunct

Dedicated to comic, rather than gender, swapping.

www.cummingfirstmethodist.com

First Cumming, Georgia, Methodist Church

www.cumstore.co.uk

Storage systems company

www.daleshitchinstation.com

Towbars, etc.

www.dicksonweb.com

Technical instrument company

www.dieselshitmen.com

Links to adult movie, sex toy, swinging etc. websites

www.dollarsexchange.com

Currency trading

For financial dealings, rather than bargain-priced gender reassignment.

www.effoff.com

Office furniture and relocation company, Effective Office Environments

www.exoticsexchange.com
Defunct

www.expertsexchange.com
Site disabled
The site address was wisely changed to Experts-Exchange.com.

www.fukhing.com
Moulding company in China

www.gamesextract.com
Artwork for video games

www.graphicartsexchange.com
Printing equipment

www.graphicsexchange.com
Graphics and web design

www.homesexchange.com
Property exchanges

www.ihavegas.com
Defunct

www.ipanywhere.com
Links to software websites

www.japan.usrelations.com
Provides links to various websites
Not to be confused with Jap-anus relations.

www.keywordsextractor.com
Defunct; site for sale

www.kidsexchange.net
Site where you can sell and buy children's clothing and toys, etc.

www.lumbermansexchange.com
Provides links to various websites

www.mammotherection.com
Scaffolding company

www.molestationnursery.com

*Site for Mole Station Native Nursery, Mole Station Tenterfield,
New South Wales, Australia, a plant company; site now called
www.molerivernursery.com*

www.momsexchange.com

Defunct; site for sale

www.MP3shits.com

MP3 music site

www.musiciansexchange.com

Defunct; site for sale

www.nice-tits.org

The former name of an ornithology site
Before it got the wrong sort of visitors. It is now a sex site.

www.northerngasheating.com
Central heating company
Do not visit if you are after someone to eat your gash.

www.nycanal.com
New York State Eerie Canal

www.oddsextractor.com
Defunct; online gambling (odds extractor)

www.palm.co.ck
Cook Island diving specialists

www.partsexpress.com
Electronic equipment

www.penisland.net
Pen Island, an online pen retailer
Its name was designed to lure customers.

www.penismightier.com
General rants
The URL was probably deliberate.

www.playersexchange.com
Defunct

www.potsofart.com
Paint your own artistic pots in Hertfordshire

www.powergenitalia.com
Under construction
It used to be the PowerGen Italia website, which later changed its name to the more prosaic www.batterychargerpowergen.it.

www.radio.co.ck
Radio Cook Islands

www.scatissue.com
A non-scatological site
Magically transfers visitors to an industrial towel company.

www.speedofart
Art direction company

www.stickersexchange.com
Bumper stickers, etc.

www.studentsexchange.com
Defunct

www.therapistfinder.com
Therapist finder

www.therapistforhire.com
Therapists for hire
Just as it says.

www.veteransexchange.com
Defunct

www.webone.com.au
Australian Internet company

www.whorepresents.com
Who Represents
A site for celebrity agents, rather than a gift site for prostitutes.

www.wintersexpress.com
Winters Express newspaper

www.womensexchange.com
Defunct; site for sale

CHAPTER 8

RIDE THE SLUT

The alphabet soup of awkward acronyms plagues organizations – according to what is most likely another urban myth, only in the nick of time did the City University of Newcastle upon Tyne decide not to use its initial letters. Others were less vigilant.

A.M.G.O.T.
Allied Military Government of Allied Territory
Coined by the British Army in 1943, but replaced by AMG when it was realized that in Turkish 'am göt' means 'cunt arse'.

A.N.U.S.
American Nihilist Underground Society;
Austrian National Union of Students

A.R.S.E.
Alabama Retired State Employees

A.S.O.L.
American Symphony Orchestras League
Changed to League of American Orchestras.

A.S.S.
Anderson Secondary School (Singapore)

B.A.P.S.
British Association of Plastic Surgeons
Among many others.

B.O.G.
Bank Officers' Guild

B.R.A.
British Rivet Association

C.L.I.T.
Command Line Interface Tool; Computer Literacy and
Internet Technology

C.O.M.E.
Centre Odontologique de Médicométrie et d'Évaluation

C.O.N.D.O.M.
College of Notre Dame of Maryland
An all-girls Catholic college.

C.R.A.P.
Canadian Reform Alliance Party

C.U.M.
Centro Universitario Metropolitano (Guatemala); Cascade Union
Metro; Communauté Urbaine de Montréal (Montreal Urban
Community, the city's former regional government organization)

C.U.M.S.
Cambridge University Musical Society

C.U.N.T.
Catholic University of North Texas; Certified Unix and Network Technician; Clean Up National Television

The last example was alleged to be the original acronym of Mary Whitehouse's Clean Up TV campaign according to the drama Filth: The Mary Whitehouse Story, *broadcast on BBC2, 29 May 2008.*

C.U.N.T.S.
Cambridge University New Testament Society; Canadian Union of Nicotine and Tobacco Sellers

D.I.C.K.
Democratic Indira Congress (Karunakaran)

D.I.L.D.O.
Direct Input Limited Duty Officer (US Navy)

F.A.R.T.
Ferrovie Autolinee Regionali Ticinesi (Regional Transport Authority for Canton Ticino, Switzerland) (and many others)

F.U.
Friends University
Allegedly F.U.C.K, Friends University of Central Kansas.

J.I.S.M.
Japanische Internationale Schule München; Jordan Institution for Standards and Metrology

N.A.D.S.
North Atlantic Defense System

N.A.L.G.A.

National Association of Local Government Auditors,
based in Lexington, Kentucky

*It changed its name to Association of Local Government Auditors
(ALGA) because* 'nalga' *in Spanish means* 'arse', *which meant
the organization was the butt of too many jokes.*

N.I.P.S.

Northern Ireland Prison Service

P.E.N.I.S.

Proton-Enhanced Nuclear Induction Spectroscopy

*United States Patent 3,792,346 (1974) for this was granted to
Michael G. Gibby, John S. Waugh and Alexander Pines – whose
surname is coincidentally an anagram of 'penis'.*

P.R.A.T.

Pharmacology Research Associate Training

S.C.R.E.W.

Special Committee to Review Extracurricular Workshops

S.H.A.G.

Senior Housing Assistance Group

S.H.I.T.

Servicio de Hosteleria Industrial de Terrassa (a shop in Terrassa,
Spain); South Hanoi Institute of Technology;
Super Huge Interferometric Telescope

S.L.U.T.

South Lake Union Trolley (Seattle)

'Ride the SLUT' T-shirts have proved a popular sideline.

S.P.E.R.M.
Social Political Economic Religious Military (a model for classifying historical events and ideas)

S.P.E.W.
Socialist Party of England and Wales

T.I.T.
Tokyo Institute for Technology

T.I.T.S.
Texas Interstate Truck Stop; Treasure Island Transit Service

T.O.O.L.
Tennessee Organization of Locksmiths

T.O.S.S.
Teachers Organization of Skill Sharing

T.W.A.T.
The War Against Terror

W.A.N.C.
Women's Auxiliary Naval Corps; Western Australian Naturalists Club; Wide Area Network Connection
The Women's Auxiliary Naval Corps was rapidly changed to Women's Royal Navy Service (WRENs).

CHAPTER 9

LOST IN
TRANSLATION

Before new enterprises and products are launched, focus groups and teams of experts are often consulted to decide on the all-important name. Despite this intense activity, all too often names that seem quite innocent in their country of origin have a totally different connotation elsewhere.

DRIVEN TO DISTRACTION

SOME VEHICLE NAMES THAT DIDN'T TRAVEL

Buick LaCrosse
In French-speaking Canada, LaCrosse means 'masturbating'.

Dodge Swinger
Despite its swinging sixties name (it was launched, aptly, in 1969), the model remained in production until the mid-1970s.

Foden
The British truck manufacturer, named after Edwin Foden (1841–1911), got into difficulties in Portugal and Brazil, where its name means 'fuck'.

Ford Fiera

Ford's truck name means 'ugly old crone' in Spanish.

Ford Pinto

The Ford Pinto was not sold in Brazil after the company realized that 'pinto' is Portuguese slang for 'small penis', and replaced it with 'corcel', a horse or steed.

Fücker

The German coach company has experienced a similar reaction in England to the one that greeted the Fokker aircraft in the Second World War.

Honda Fitta

Unsaleable in Scandinavia, where 'fitta' is slang for vagina (in Swedish, Norwegian and Danish).

Mazda LaPuta

Laputa is also the name of a fabulous flying island in Jonathan Swift's Gulliver's Travels. 'Puta' is also Spanish for prostitute. According to Mazda's advertising campaign, their 'LaPuta is designed to deliver maximum utility in a minimum space while providing a smooth, comfortable ride'.

Mercury Comet Caliente

In Portuguese, 'caliente' means hot in the sense of horny – a 'caliente' is a streetwalker in Brazil.

Mitsubishi Pajero

In Spanish a 'pajero' is a masturbator – the name was therefore changed to Montero.

Nissan Moco

'Moco' is Spanish for 'mucus' or 'bogy'.

Opel Ascona

'Ascona' is Spanish and Portuguese for 'female genitalia'.

Rolls-Royce Silver Mist
The Silver Shadow was so-called before the company realized 'mist' means 'shit' in German.

Toyota MR2
Its name is pronounced as 'em-er-deux' in French, hence sounds like 'merde', 'shit'.

ALL AT SEA

Ship names, such as *Clit I*, and *Tits*, the yacht owned by Prince Jefri Bolkiah of Brunei and since renamed *Samax*, with two tenders, *Nipple I* and *Nipple II*, are often contrived, but *Master Baiter*, a lobster boat in Pemaquid, Maine, USA, may be accidentally funny, as is *Titan Uranus*, a 137,746-ton crude oil tanker, built in 1992 and owned by Singapore-based Titan Ocean company. A number of Royal Navy vessels have received embarrassing names, among them HMS *Fairy*, *Frolic*, *Pansy*, *Sappho* and *Spanker*, while US Navy vessels include USS *Flasher*, *Ponce* and *Uranus*.

RUDE FOOD

The subject of a number of excellent books, such as Rosie Walford et al's *Shelf Life* (London: Bloomsbury, 2004) and websites, most notably *Rude Food* (currently in limbo, but archived at www.dazbert.co.uk/sites/rudefoodold), where some of these and many more examples are delightfully depicted, this offers a taster menu of food products whose names meant they were destined not to travel beyond their countries of origin.

Aass
Norwegian brewer and soft drinks company

Bender
Chicken burger produced by Wimpy
A Bender in a bun and a Bender with cheese are optional.

Big Nuts
KP product marketed in a variety of flavours
A Belgian chocolate-covered version is also available.

Bog
Danish tinned meat product

Bonka
Coffee brand marketed by Nestlé in Spain

Bum
Popular brand of Spanish crisps

Bum Bum
French banana-flavoured ice cream lolly served with a stick of chewing gum

Bundh sauces
Made by Sharwoods
In the Punjab 'Bundh' sounds like the word for 'arse'.

Chilito
When Taco Bell discovered that its new chilli burrito product was Mexican slang for 'penis', it was changed to Chilo Burrito.

Chilli Willy
Californian-made hot chilli sauce
A British company of the same name supplies penis-shaped chillies to enable you to grow your own.

Cock
Thai cooking sauce, a Jamaican soup mix and
numerous other products

Cockburns
Well-known British port
Pronounced Co-burns, as any fule kno...

French bacon-flavoured corn snack

Coming
Japanese lemon-flavoured sweet

Cool-Piss
Korean carbonated yogurt drink

Coq Fromage
French dish of turkey combined with cheese
Literally translated as 'cock cheese'.

Coq Prime
French coffee
Has a French cock as its logo.

Crap's
French chocolate bar

Cream Collon
Japanese sweets

Creamy Ball
Japanese chocolate-flavoured balls

Dickmilch
German milk-based product

Dorset Knob
Traditional British biscuit

Romanian energy drink containing the high-caffeine
plant extract guarana

Faggs
Coffee from New Zealand
*Despite its name, it is promoted under the banner
'The great straight coffee'.*

Peruvian strawberry jam brand; also the name of a Finnish chocolate dessert and a Spanish orange company

Fartons
Sweet snack from Spain

Finger Marie
McVitie's rich tea biscuits, as sold in Sweden

Fizzy Jerkz
British sweets from the Wonka line

Friggs
Swedish manufacturers of rice bread

Grated Fanny
Tinned tuna marketed in Aruba

Happy Crak
Spanish popcorn

Hardon
Tea brand from Curaçao

Horn
Japanese chocolate

Fresca
Soft drink
*This product is widely sold – except in Mexico, where
'fresca' means 'lesbian'.*

Gits
Variety of poppadom from India

Gros Jos
*The US food company Hunt-Wesson initially sold its 'Big John'
products in Canada under the brand name 'Gros Jos' – which is
French Canadian slang for 'a woman with large breasts'.*

Brand of homogenized milk in Canada

Jussipussi
Finnish bread product made by Primula

Kocky
Portuguese milk drink

Finnish crisps

Muffs
Brazilian cakes

Nips
Hard candy manufactured in the USA by Nestlé

Nobbys Nuts
Australian salted beer nuts
The slogan 'Nibble Nobby's Nuts!' may be deliberate.

Pee Cola
Ghanaian soft drink

Plopp
Swedish chocolate bar

Prick
Brazilian crisps

Pussi
Swedish catfood

Pussi Milk
Milk from Sweden

Ghanaian hot pepper sauce

Sissy
Chilean biscuits

Skum
Swedish confectionery

Dutch beer

Slagroom
Dutch whipped cream

SorBits
Mints available in Scandinavia

Spunk
Danish salt-flavoured liquorice

Spurty Bones
German bones (for dogs)

Squirt
Guatemalan carbonated drink

Vergina
Macedonian lager

Wanker
US beer
All its labels feature scantily clad women.

ASIAN FOOD IS PRETTY RUDE

Almost all Thai and much other Asian food is pretty rude –
a typical menu might offer:

Bangus

Hor fun

Khao pad prik gai

Ma ho

Phat prik ho

Pupu

Tod man poo

OTHER PRODUCTS AND COMPANIES

Like the car models above, some company names
just don't work in other countries.

Analtech

Chromatography company based in Newark, Delaware, USA

Arçelik

Turkish refrigerator manufacturer

Bardak

Machinery company
*Would perhaps have difficulty breaking into the Russian market,
where its name means 'whorehouse'.*

Butt Drilling

Company in Springlands, New Zealand

Colgate Cue

This toothpaste was not sold in France, where 'cue' *means* 'arse'.

Cona

Cona Coffee Machine Co.
*Named after its founder Alfred Cohn, the company was
unable to sell its products in Portugal, where* 'cona' *means
'cunt'. In Portuguese-speaking countries it is marketed under the
name Acolon.*

Dirty Dick's Crab House

Restaurant chain in Virginia, Florida and North Carolina, USA

Farto

Pharmacist shop in São Paulo, Brazil

Fu King
Chinese Restaurant, Lake City, Florida

Fuk Mi
Sushi and seafood buffet
Allegedly in Malaysia, but almost certainly an Internet hoax.

GPT
Joint venture by Plessy and GEC in France
In France, GPT is said as 'j'ai pété', meaning 'I have farted'.

Ikea Fartfull
*After a range of products with names such as Bøg and Dik,
Ikea's Fartfull desk was less than popular in
English-speaking territories.*

Jotter
*The Parker pen was not sold in parts of South America
where a 'jotter' is slang for a 'jockstrap'.*

I ♥ cum
*As a result of weird typography, the newspaper Christmas
greeting placed by Swedish company Locum in 2001 appeared
to read quite differently.*

Mensa
Club for the super-intelligent
Except in Spain, where a 'mensa' is a 'stupid woman'.

Hotel Moron
Ciego de Avila, Cuba; Cala Ratjada, Mallorca, Spain, etc.

Mammoth Erections
Company based in Austin, Texas

My Dung

Restaurant, Rosemead, California

Osram

Manufacturer of light bulbs and electronic control gear
In Polish the word 'osram' *means 'to shit on something'.*

Pansy

Chinese male underwear brand
Unsurprisingly this brand has yet to catch on in the West.

Pledge

Johnson Company's polish brand
Presumably would prove less popular to shoppers in the Netherlands, where its name means 'piss'.

Puffs

Tissues
Not in Germany, where 'puff' *means 'brothel'.*

Skinny Dick's Half-Way Inn

A restaurant between Ester and Nenana, Alaska, USA

Superglans

Dutch car shampoo and wax

Super Piss

Finnish lock de-icer

Tits

Woman's fashion shop, Montevideo, Uruguay

Trim Pecker

Japanese trousers brand

Wack Off

Australian insect repellent

CHAPTER 10

THE WONDERFUL WORLD OF SCIENCE AND NATURE

It's not all serious work in the lab – even science represents a fertile source of amusingly rude names.

Arsenolite (As$_2$O$_3$)
The mineral, cubic arsenic trioxide

Arsole
The Dow Chemical Company's US patent number 3,412,119 is entitled 'Substituted Stannoles, Phospholes, Arsoles, and Stiboles'

Arsole is also the subject of a 1983 paper by G. Markl and H. Hauptmann and J. Organomet, 'Studies on the Chemistry of the Arsoles'.

Bastard balm
(*Melittis melissophyllum*)

Bastard cabbage
(*Rapistrum rugosum* ssp. *rugosum*)

Bastard service tree
(*Sorbus* x *thuringiaca*)

Black man's willy
(*Rhodochiton atrosanguineus* or *Rhodochiton volubilis*)
Also known as the purple bell vine
It was referred to on the BBC4 radio programme Gardeners'
Question Time, *broadcast from the Chilcompton Gardening*
Club, Somerset, on 7 October 2007, in which plantswoman Anne
Swithinbank commented, 'I've never seen one in my life. They
don't really like the cold, as you can imagine. They shrivel up
and look very unhappy.' This resulted in an official apology
(5 February 2008).

Clitoriacetal
Named after the *Clitoria macrophylla* plant, from the
roots of which it is derived
It is a constituent of a drug for treating respiratory ailments.

Clitorin
A flavenol glycoside

Cockhold herb
(*Bidens connata*)

Cox-Zucker machine
An algorithm
*First described by David Cox and Stephen Zucker in 1979 and
so-named by C. F. Schwartz in a mathematics paper in 1984.*

Cuckoo pint
(*Arum maculatum*)
The 'pint' part of its name comes from the Anglo Saxon for 'penis'.

Dickite ($Al_2Si_2O_5(OH)_4$)
A mineral
Named after Scottish chemist, Alan Brugh Dick (1833–1926).

Donkey dong
(*Holothuria mexicana*)
A kind of sea cucumber
Resembles an ass's appendage.

Erectone
One of several compounds extracted from the herb
Hypericum erectum
*It is used in traditional Chinese medicine to treat stiffness –
of the joints.*

Fuchsite ($KAl_2(AlSi_3O_{10})(F,OH)_2$)
A mineral, the green form of Muscovite

Fucitol ($C_6H_{14}O_5$)
Derived from *Fucus vesiculosus*, a seaweed;
Fucitol is a type of alcohol

Fucol
A sugar that can be extracted from the eggs of sea urchins,
frog spawn and milk

Fukalite ($Ca_4Si_2O_6(CO_3)(OH,F)_2$)
A mineral named after Fuka, Japan

Fukiic acid

*'Fuki', the Japanese word for the butterbur flower,
gives the acid derived from it its name and that of another
product, Fukinolic acid*

Fukuchilite (Cu_3FeS_8)

A mineral
*Named after Japanese mineralogist Nobuyo Fukuchi
(1877–1934).*

Fukugetin

Found in the bark of the Garcenia tree
*Also known as Morellofavone and its glucoside is
called Fukugiside.*

Fungus stinkhorn

(*Phallus impudicus*)

Knobweed

(*Hyptis capitata*)
James Cook University's online dictionary of plants describes
knobweed as 'woody and erect…'.

Nipplewort

(*Lapsana communis*)
It was once recommended for treating breast ulcers.

Rubus cockburnianus

'Strong growing, upright, thorny purple stems'.

Shagbark hickory

(*Carya ovata*)

Slippery Dick

(*Halichoeres bivittatus*)
A member of the wrasse fish family
It grows to about 8–12 inches.

Sticky willy

(*Galium aparine*)

Stiff cock
(*Diospyros crassenevis*)
*Its leaves are used to make tea that is claimed to have
aphrodisiac properties.*

THE END